Research Methods

for OCR Psychology

Beth Black & Cara Flanagan

'All you need to know!'

Published in 2005 by:
Nelson Thornes Ltd
Delta Place
27 Bath Road
CHELTENHAM
GL53 7TH
United Kingdom

05 06 07 08 09 / 10 9 8 7 6 5 4 3 2 1

A catalogue record for this book is available from the British Library

ISBN 0 7487 9435 2

Illustrations by Rupert Besley, IFA Design and Angela Lumley
Page make-up by IFA Design

Printed in Croatia by Zrinski

Acknowledgements

The author and publishers are grateful to the
following for permission to reproduce photographs
and other copyright material in this book:

OCR examination questions are reproduced by
kind permission of OCR; Clegg, Simple Statistics:
A Course Book for Students, 1983, Cambridge
University Press p.142; FACS coding table
reproduced by permission of Joseph C.Hager,
A Human Face. P.56; Runyon, Fundamentals of
Behavioural Statistics, McGraw-Hill. Reproduced
by permission of the McGraw-Hill Companies
p.140; Innocents struggle with life after jail,
reproduced by permission of © Guardian
Newspapers Ltd p.110; KaSo 12 graphs
reproduced by permission of University Psychiatric
Services, Laupenstrasse 49, CH-3010 Bern,
Switzerland p.55;Table 1, p.579 from significance
ranking of the Spearman Rank Correlation
Coefficient by Z.H. Zhar, pp.578-90, Vol. 67,
No.339, September 1972. Reprinted with
permission from The Journal of the American
Statistical Association. All rights reserved p.139.

Photo credits:

Advertising Archive, p.100; Aidan Bell, p.47;
Alamy, pp.27, 30; Alamy/Bill Brookes, p.31;
Alamy/Klovenback, p.25;Alamy/Oote Boe Inc,
p.31;Albert Bandura, p.23;© Alexandra Milgram,
pp.27, 30; Carol Gilligan, p.40;CartoonStock,
p.116;From John Henry and his Mighty Hammer
by Rozanne Litzinger. Copyright © 1994 by Troll
Communications. Reprinted by permission of
Scholastic Inc, p.34; Martin Sookias, p.109;
Newcast/Camelot, p.12; Nick Kim, p.42;
PA/ABACA/Empics, p.116; Philip Zimbardo,
Psychology Department, Stanford University,
p.60; Photolibrary/Foodpix/Evan Sklar, p.80;
Powerstock/Age Fotostock, p.4; Retna
Pictures/Andrew Kent. p.11; Rex Features/Mark
Campbell, p.73; Richard Duszczak Cartoon
Studio Limited, p.39; Ronald Grant Archive, p.54;
Shout Picture Library, p.81; The Far Side, Gary
Larsen/Creators Syndicate, p.32;
www.york.ac.uk/depts/maths/histstat/people/,p.139.

Royalty free:

Corbis Royalty free p.101 (both); Corbis V94 (NT)
p.91; Corbis V198 (NT) p.72; Corel 155 (NT) p.1;
Corel 250 (NT) pp.14,43; Corel 283 (NT) p.1;
Corel 642 (NT) p.91; Corel 654 (NT) p.64; Corel
656 (NT) p.25; Corel 713 (NT) p.73; Image 100
EE (NT) pp.33,52; Photodisc 2 (NT) p.56 (both);
Photodisc 6 (NT) p.26; Photodisc 10 (NT) p.44;
Photodisc 28 (NT) p.2; Photodisc 41 (NT) p.12;
Photodisc 44 (NT) p.26 (both); Photodisc 45 (NT)
pp.20,118; Photodisc 46 (NT) p.88; Photodisc
50 (NT) pp.6,46; Photodisc 56 (NT) p.24;
Photodisc 73 (NT) pp.1,14,65; Photodisc 76 (NT)
p79; Rubberball WW (NT) p.8; Tom LeGoff/Digital
Vision HU (NT) p.16.

Every effort has been made to contact copyright
holders, and we apologise if any have been
overlooked. Should copyright have been unwittingly
infringed in this book, the owners should contact
the publishers, who will make corrections at
reprint.

Contents

Beatrix

Dedications

To Beatrix and Andrew (and many others) for putting up with me. BB

To Philippa (who kept me company over the hot summer during which I wrote the bulk of this book). Thanks too to the rest of the family: Rob and Jack, and Rosie (who asked the question that starts the book, see page 1). CF

Acknowledgements

First and foremost a huge thanks to Hugh Coolican for answering all our picky questions with picky answers, and always being ready to help.

Thanks also to so many different people who have contributed ideas, jokes, comments … Adrian Frost, Sara Berman, Julia Russell, and those unsung others from whom we have stolen ideas and forgotten the source.

And finally the team at Nelson Thornes have provided the enthusiastic backup we have come to expect: Rick Jackman, Nigel Harriss and Vanessa Thompson who are such a delight to work with.

Special thanks to the guinea pigs

This book has benefited enormously from the feedback given by the teachers and students of Bristol City College (Tony Willner, Maria Kamba and Lana Crosbie), Claires Court School (Sara Berman) and St. Mary Redcliffe & Temple School (Grace Pittman and Rob Endley). They kindly had a go at using the first draft of this book and gave us invaluable feedback.

How to use this book

This book is divided into two parts.

Part 1. A short course in research methods, with lots of mini-activities and questions to help understanding. You can use this material to support students in producing their Practical Investigations Folder and to prepare students for the Psychological Investigations AS examination (2542).

Part 2. Specific instructions related to exam work: the AS Practical Investigations Folder, the AS Psychological Investigations exam (2542) and the A2 coursework (2543). There are ideas for activities, examples of student practical investigations folders, practical projects and assignments, plus examiner's advice on how to prepare these, and also examples of exam questions for the AS Psychological Investigations exam with student answers and examiner's comments

There are two ways that students can use this book:

Method I – Read about a research method presented in Part 1 of the book, and then tackle the related Pratical Investigation Activity in Part 2 of the book.

Method II – Decide on a Practical Investigation Activity (described in Part 2) and access relevant knowledge about research methods and design considerations by dipping into the wealth of material in Part 1.

This book doesn't cover everything there is to know about research methods in psychology but intends to do enough for the OCR specification. An understanding of research methods is essential for OCR Psychology, not only for the Psychological Investigations exam, but also in order to evaluate the strengths and weaknesses of the Core Studies and research in the A2 part of the course. Some of the AS Core Studies appear throughout Part 1 of the book as a way of helping students understand a particular research method or issue.

This book aims to provide a thorough understanding of the required concepts. Some users have commented that there is too much depth in some areas, but this has been necessary in order to ensure that students do understand what often appear to be deceptively simple concepts. Students and teachers who have used this book report that the activities made them think a lot, that they felt they really came to understood research methods, and they found the book interesting and humourous!

Sit back and enjoy yourself while improving your examination marks.

EXTRAS

There is an OCR student workbook to go with this book.

Students can use this to record details of all the terms in the book and then use this booklet for revision. You can download this booklet from the Nelson Thornes website.

Also available is a set of answers to all the questions **Qs** in pink boxes.

And you can obtain, from the website, a word file containing templates for certain activities (those marked 🖥).

Introduction

The other day, Cara's daughter Rosie said to her, 'So what is it psychologists do?', and Cara answered that they try to explain why people do certain things.

Rosie's next question was, 'How do they do that?'

The answer is that they do research studies to test their beliefs about why people do the things they do.

Cara's daughter Rosie.

One way to conduct research is to ask people why they do what they do, or ask them what they think and feel. This method of conducting research is called an **interview**.

We will look at how to conduct interviews in Chapter 3.

Or they could write a **questionnaire** containing a variety of questions.

This research method is also looked at in Chapter 3.

Another way to conduct research is to watch what people do. This method of conducting research is called an **observation** or observational study.

We will look at observational studies in Chapter 4.

If we want to know what causes people to do certain things, we have to conduct an **experiment**.

There are different kinds of experiment, which are the topic of Chapters 1 and 2.

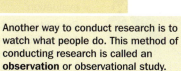

Qs   1

1. Think about how you might conduct your own research.

   The topic is television advertisements. The question is 'What adverts are most effective?'. Suggest **two or more** ways in which you might investigate this research question.

2. What would be the aim of this research?

*Every study has a **research aim** – what it is that the researcher wants to find out, which may include one or more research questions.*

All of these are **research methods** – a way of finding things out in a systematic manner.

Once we have decided on a **method**, we need to **design** the particulars.

Research design is like designing a room – it is the plan of what you are going to do.
Try to bear this in mind – there are research methods and research designs (experimental design, the design of observations, the design of questionnaires, etc.).

These are all bathrooms – but each one has a different **design**.

Symbols used in this book

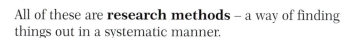

Qs   1

On most spreads, there are questions for you to answer.
Suggested answers can be found at www.nelsonthornes.com/researchmethods

ctivity 1   **A simple experiment:**

Activities are indicated with this symbol and sometimes accompanied by this icon which indicates that the materials can be found on the website if you wish to print extra copies.

The box on the right identifies the terms (key terms and other terms) that you should record notes on in your OCR student workbook, which can be found on the Nelson Thornes website. When you have finished this book, you will have a set of revision notes that you have made.

KEY TERMS
Key terms to record
(these are terms that you must know):
   Aims
   Research design
   Research method

Symbol indicates that this is a core study for the AS Core Studies 1 and 2 examinations

Research methods and your exams

There are two ways that research methods are examined in the OCR specification: indirectly and directly.

Directly
AS level: Psychological investigations exam
A2 level: Coursework

Indirectly
Your knowledge of research methods is also examined in all your other Psychology examinations, both at AS (in Core Studies 1 and Core Studies 2) as well as in the two A2 units you will do. This is because a major way of evaluating any study is by being able to discuss methodological strengths and weaknesses.

AS level exams: Research methods questions

In both Core Studies examinations, many questions will specifically target your ability to be able to spot a methodological flaw or weakness in a study.

A2 level exams: Research methods questions

In your A2 examinations, some questions may specifically ask you to evaluate psychological research from a methodological point of view (and some ask you to 'evaluate' something), in which case you may choose the 'evaluation issues'. Common and successful evaluation issues include:

- Ecological validity
- Sample and generalisability
- Validity of the research
- Reliability of the research

At AS and A2 your knowledge of research methods gives you a useful set of tools with which to evaluate and analyse, dissect and pick apart the research which you will learn about

Some example of questions from A2 units specifically targeting research methods:

Psychology and Environment Section A
1. (a) Describe **one** study of personal space. (6)
   (b) Evaluate the ethics of researching personal space. (10)

Psychology and Health Section A
1. (a) Describe **one** way of measuring adherence to medical advice. (6)
   (b) Evaluate the methods of measuring adherence to medical advice. (10)

Psychology and Education Section A
1. (a) Describe **one** psychological study of the effects of classroom design on educational performance. (6)
   (b) Evaluate the methods of researching the effects of classroom design on educational performance. (10)

Psychology and Organisations Section A
1. (a) Describe **one** psychometric test used in organisations. (6)
   (b) Discuss the validity of psychometric testing in organisations. (10)

Some examples of questions involving a methodological evaluation:

Core Studies 1
1. (a) Briefly describe the experimental and control group in the study on brain scanning by Raine, Buchsbaum and LaCasse. (2)
   (b) Explain why Raine, Buchsbaum and LaCasse used a control group. (2)
2. Describe **one** ethical and **one** practical problem in Hodges and Tizard's study of social relationships. (4)
3. Describe **one** advantage and **one** disadvantage of conducting a field experiment as shown in the subway Samaritan study by Piliavin, Rodin and Piliavin. (4)

Core Studies 2 (Section A)
Ecological validity refers to whether psychological research is related to everyday life. It is often difficult to carry out ecologically valid research in a laboratory. Choose **one** of the core studies listed below and answer the following questions.
   Haney, Banks and Zimbardo (prison simulation)
   Tajfel (intergroup discrimination)
   Dement and Kleitman (sleep and dreaming)
(a) Describe the procedure of your chosen study. (6)
(b) Using examples, give **four** ways in which your chosen study was low in ecological validity. (12)
(c) Suggest **one** way in which the ecological validity of your chosen study could be improved and say how you think this might affect the results. (8)

Core Studies 2 (Section B)
One common way of collecting data in psychology is to ask participants questions and then to analyse the answers. Such data are referred to as a self-report measure.
Each of the studies listed below used self-report measures.
   Hraba and Grant (doll choice)
   Hodges and Tizard (social relationships)
   Thigpen and Cleckley (multiple personality disorder)
   Schachter and Singer (emotion)
(a) Describe the self-report measure that was used in each of these studies. (12)
(b) Using examples from these studies, discuss **two** strengths and **two** weaknesses of using self report-measures (12)

AS exam (Unit 2542): Psychological investigations

This is a one hour exam. It is worth 16.67% of your final A level mark.

The exam is divided into **four sections**, each based on one of the activities in your **practical investigations folder** (see below). There tend to be three types of question in the exam.

- Some of these questions involve copying directly from your practical investigations folder. If your booklet is incomplete or lacking in detail, you will lose precious marks!

- Some questions will ask you about your activity but not involve copying – they may be about problems or weaknesses, or different ways of conducting the activity.

- Some questions may ask you about more methodological issues.

There is guidance about answering these exam questions in Chapter 5.

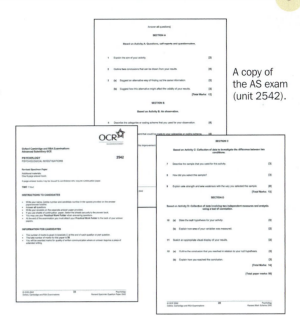

A copy of the AS exam (unit 2542).

A2 assessment (Unit 2543) Coursework

There are two written pieces of coursework you need to produce. Jointly they are worth 16.6% of your final A level mark.

1. The Practical Project

2. The Assignment

The Practical Project

The report should be a maximum of 1400 words long and is based on some research you have conducted yourself.

The Assignment

The report should be a maximum of 1000 words in length. The purpose of the assignment is to see if you can use psychological knowledge to help explain real life events as recounted in a newspaper or magazine article.

Detailed instructions about both of these are given in Chapter 6.

The practical investigations folder

Candidates should be provided with a folder containing suitable headings. They fill this in with the details of four practical investigations that they have conducted:

Activity A: Questions, self-reports and questionnaires (see pages 64–65 for examples of what to do).

Activity B: An observation (see pages 72–73 for examples of what to do).

Activity C: Collection of data to investigate the difference between two conditions (see pages 80–81 for examples of what to do).

Activity D: Collection of data involving independent measures and analysed using a test of correlation (see pages 88–89 for examples of what to do).

For each activity you are required to record details such as the aims, hypothesis, variables, sample, procedures, analysis and conclusions.

A template for the practical investigations folder is provided on the website for this book: www.nelsonthornes.com/researchmethods

Your folder will not be marked by the exam board but you will use it in the written examination.

Where to look in this book:	
Written exam: Psychological investigations	Possible questions are shown on pages 70, 78, 86 and 94. Some model answers on pages 71, 79, 87 and 95.
The practical investigations folder	Instructions on filling this in for each activity are given on pages 66, 74, 82 and 90. Model folders for each activity are shown on pages 67, 75, 83 and 91.
The practical project	Details are given on pages 98-107, including a Grade A and a Grade C example of a Practical Project.
The assignment	Details are given on pages 108-117, including a Grade A and a Grade C example of an Assignment.
AS exam questions relating to research methods	Questions are given on pages 125-129.
A2 exam questions relating to research methods	Questions are given on pages 130-131.

Contents

Experiments

What is an experiment?

An experiment is a way of conducting research where:

One **variable** is made to change (by the experimenter)

(this is called the **independent variable** or **IV**).

The effects of the IV on another variable are observed or measured

(this variable is called the **dependent variable** or **DV**).

> You actually know all about experiments – you conduct them without thinking. For example, when you start a new class with a new teacher, you see how he or she responds to your behaviour – you might make a joke or hand your homework in on time (both IVs) to see whether the teacher responds well (the DV). You are experimenting with cause and effect.

A variable is just a thing – something that can change. For example, noise is a variable. It can be soft or loud.

Activity 1 — A simple experiment: Does noise affect memory?

The variable we are going to change (the **IV**) is noise.

The variable we are going to measure (the **DV**) is performance on a memory task.

You will need a radio and two lists of 20 words each. You can use the right-hand wordlist on page 16. There are 40 words in the list.

Divide your class in half: Group N (noise) and Group S (silent).

Group N should have the radio playing very loudly when they are shown the list of words. They have 1 minute to try to remember them and then 1 minute to write them down.

Group S should do the same task, in silence, with the second list of words.

Which group remembered most words?

And another experiment: Is performance affected by expectation?

If you want people to perform better, does it help to lie to them about the quality of materials they are using? Do people perform better if they think the materials they are using are better?

A study by Weick *et al.* (1973) tested this by telling two jazz bands (Band A and Band B) that the piece of music they were rehearsing was either (1) by a composer whose work was well respected or (2) by a composer whose work had been negatively reviewed. Weick *et al.* found that people performed better if they thought they were playing a well-respected work. Participants also remembered the piece better and liked it better.

However, this finding might be because Band A was actually a better band than Band B. To overcome this problem, the experiment was designed so that both bands played both musical pieces: Piece 1 and Piece 2.

Band A was told that Piece 1 was by the superior composer and Piece 2 was by the inferior composer.

Band B was told that Piece 1 was by the inferior composer and Piece 2 was by the superior composer.

Many things that are called experiments are actually investigations. An experiment must have an IV and a DV.

Qs — 2

1. Think of some other variables, and for each say how they can vary.
2. Does noise affect your memory?
   a. What was the IV?
   b. What was the DV?
   c. What was the aim of this experiment?
3. Drunken goldfish
   a. What was the IV?
   b. What was the DV?
4. Is performance affected by expectation?
   a. What was the IV?
   b. What was the DV?
   c. What was the aim of this experiment?

Another experiment: Drunken goldfish

Many early psychology experiments focused on learning in animals. The learning involved simple mazes where the animal was rewarded if it turned in the desired direction at the end of a maze shaped like a Y.

In one experiment, goldfish were trained in a maze and afterwards placed in a water solution high in alcohol. Some of them keeled over.

When the goldfish were retested a week later, those goldfish who had not been exposed to alcohol could remember the maze task perfectly, but those who blacked out in the alcohol solution had no memory for the task. This demonstrates the severe effects of alcohol on learning (Ryback, 1969).

Psychology has been plagued by many foolish experiments – of which this is one. Don't try it at home.

KEY TERMS
Experiment
Dependent variable
Independent variable

Activity 2 — **Reading in colour – the Stroop effect**

Students should work in pairs. One person (the participant) reads the word lists while the other person (the experimenter) times how long it takes to read each list (all mobile phones have timers so this should be easy to arrange!).

Instructions:

1 Participants should read the practice list first so both participant and experimenter can practise what they have to do:

- Cover up lists 1–4.

- Participants should state the colour of the word, not what the word says. For example, for the word 'BLUE' they should say 'red', for the word 'BROWN' they should say 'brown'.

- Participants should take great care to say the colour correctly and not race against the clock. Mistakes should be corrected.

- The experimenter should check that the words are read correctly. In order to do this, a non-colour version is printed below.

- The experimenter says 'start' to signal to the participant to begin reading the first list.

- The participant says 'stop' at the end of the list, so the experimenter can record how long it took to read the list.

2 Participants should now read the remaining lists. Each time, they should cover up the other lists and follow the same instructions as above.

Practice	List 1	List 2	List 3	List 4
green	blue	blue	green	red
blue	red	green	purple	blue
brown	brown	purple	blue	green
red	purple	red	green	red
blue	blue	brown	blue	brown
brown	green	red	brown	blue
green	brown	blue	purple	green
blue	red	green	red	purple
brown	blue	brown	blue	brown
purple	purple	purple	green	red
blue	red	brown	blue	purple
green	green	purple	red	blue
purple	brown	red	brown	purple
green	green	blue	purple	brown
purple	brown	red	green	purple
red	purple	green	brown	blue
blue	red	blue	purple	green
purple	blue	brown	red	brown
red	brown	purple	brown	blue
green	green	green	red	brown
purple	blue	purple	blue	red
blue	purple	red	purple	green
red	red	green	brown	red
green	green	blue	green	brown
red	brown	red	purple	green
brown	green	brown	blue	purple
blue	purple	blue	red	red
green	red	green	brown	blue
brown	blue	brown	green	purple
blue	purple	purple	red	green
stop	stop	stop	stop	stop

Practice	List 1	List 2	List 3	List 4
brown	red	blue	green	brown
green	blue	green	purple	red
red	green	purple	blue	brown
purple	brown	red	green	purple
red	purple	brown	blue	green
brown	blue	red	brown	purple
green	red	blue	purple	brown
blue	brown	green	red	brown
red	green	brown	blue	red
blue	red	purple	green	purple
purple	purple	brown	blue	green
red	red	purple	red	brown
purple	blue	red	brown	green
green	brown	blue	purple	red
purple	purple	red	green	blue
red	red	green	brown	purple
green	green	blue	purple	red
red	purple	brown	red	green
purple	blue	purple	brown	red
green	purple	green	red	blue
purple	brown	purple	blue	green
blue	green	red	purple	brown
green	brown	green	brown	blue
brown	red	blue	green	purple
blue	green	red	purple	blue
purple	purple	brown	blue	red
blue	brown	blue	red	green
green	blue	green	brown	purple
brown	purple	brown	green	blue
purple	blue	purple	red	brown
stop	stop	stop	stop	stop

When you have finished, turn the page for the next step …

A debriefing

You no doubt realized that in lists 1 and 4, the colour words were written in conflicting colours, which made these lists take longer to read than lists 2 and 3. This is called *The Stroop effect* after a study first conducted by J. Ridley Stroop in 1935. You can read his original article at http://psychclassics.yorku.ca/Stroop/.

Qs 3

1. What was the IV?
2. What was the DV?
3. What were the aims of this experiment?
4. Did you guess what the aims of the experiment were?
5. Draw a bar chart to show your class findings.

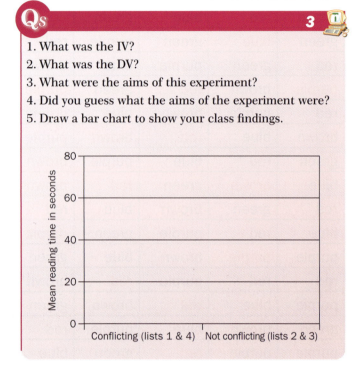

People who take part in an experiment are called **participants**. *Psychologists used to use the term 'subjects'.*

Explanation of the Stroop effect

The interference between the different information (what the words say and the colour of the words) that your brain receives causes a problem. One way to explain this is in terms of automatic processing – we read words automatically so when trying to name the colours, we cannot help but read the words, and this causes interference.

A way to test this is to see if children who are only just learning to read have as much difficulty with the task. They can read the words, but reading is not yet an automatic activity and therefore they are not as affected by the conflict. Try this out on some small children who know their colours but cannot yet read! We would imagine that the children would not get confused by this puzzle because the words would not be read automatically. Research studies support this expectation.

The Stroop effect is not just an interesting phenomenon, it is also useful. It is used to identify people with brain-damage because they find the task more difficult than non-brain-damaged people.

Stroop's findings

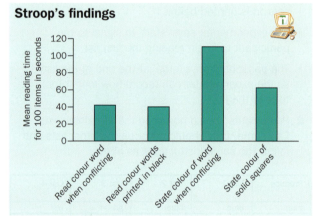

Pilot studies

If you tried one or more of the experiments, you were probably aware that there were flaws. Did you realize beforehand that there would be flaws? Or did some of the flaws become apparent after conducting the experiment? If you did not try these experiments, can you think what flaws there might be?

It is always a good idea to conduct a **pilot study** before the experiment proper. A pilot study is a small-scale trial of a research design run before doing the real thing. It is done in order to find out whether certain things do not work. For example, participants may not understand the instructions or they may guess what the experiment is about, or they may get very bored because there are too many tasks or too many questions.

Qs 4

Consider that the experiments you have conducted were pilot studies.

Suggest one thing you might change about each of the experiments so they worked better.

KEY TERMS

Pilot study

Hypotheses

A **hypothesis** states what you believe to be true. It is a precise and testable statement of the relationship between two variables.

The hypothesis for Stroop's experiment is:

'People take longer to state the colour of a word when it is written in a conflicting colour than when the word and the colour it is written in are the same.'

OR *'It takes longer to read a list of conflicting words than non-conflicting words.'*

The hypothesis is sometimes called the **experimental hypothesis** (H^1) or the **alternative hypothesis** (alternative to the null hypothesis H_0).

A hypothesis is not the same as the research aims.

When writing your own hypothesis it is essential that you say how the variables were measured or manipulated. This is called operationalisation -see page 13.

Qs 5

1. Write a hypothesis for the experiment on noise and performance on a memory task.

2. State whether your hypothesis is directional or non-directional and explain why you chose this kind of hypothesis.

3. What were the aims of this experiment?

4. For each of the following, decide whether it is a directional or a non-directional hypothesis:

   a. Boys score differently on aggressiveness tests from girls.

   b. Students who have a computer at home do better in exams than those who do not.

   c. People remember the words that appear early in a list better than the words that appear later.

   d. People given a list of emotionally charged words recall less than participants given a list of emotionally neutral words.

   e. Hamsters are better pets than budgies.

   f. Words presented in a written form are recalled differently from those presented in a pictorial form.

5. Now write your own. For each of the following experiments, write a directional and a non-directional hypothesis, and a null hypothesis:

   a. A study to find out whether girls watch more television than boys.

   b. A study to see whether teachers give more attractive students higher marks on essays than students who are less attractive.

   c. A study to investigate whether lack of sleep affects schoolwork.

Directional and non-directional hypotheses

A **directional hypothesis** states the kind of difference or relationship between two conditions or two groups of participants.

A **non-directional hypothesis** simply predicts that there will be a difference or relationship between two conditions or two groups of participants.

Directional — People take *longer* to state the colour of a word when it is written in a conflicting colour than when the word and the colour it is written in are the same.

Non-directional — Performance speeds are *different* when people state the colour of a word when it is written in a conflicting colour than when the word and the colour it is written in are the same.

Directional — People who do homework *without* the TV on produce *better* results than those who do homework with the TV on.

Non-directional — There is a *difference* between work produced in noisy or silent conditions.

One-tailed and two-tailed

Some people say 'one-tailed' instead of 'directional' and 'two-tailed' instead of 'non-directional'. When you look at a one-tailed cat you know which way it is going.

The null hypothesis (H_0)

In some circumstances (that you don't need to bother about), there is a need to state a null hypothesis – this is a statement of *no difference* or *no relationship* between the variables.

For example:

- There is no difference between work produced in noisy or silent conditions.

- There is no relationship between age and intelligence.

Why have directions?

Justifying the use of directional and non-directional hypotheses

Why do psychologists sometimes use a directional hypothesis instead of a non-directional one?

Psychologists use a directional hypothesis when past research (theory or study) suggests that the findings will go in a particular direction.

Psychologists use a non-directional hypothesis when past research is unclear or contradictory.

KEY TERMS

Null hypothesis
Hypothesis

NOTE: A hypothesis should concern populations and not samples. These concepts are explained on page 10.

Repeated measures and independent groups design

The experiment on noise and memory is an example of an **independent groups design.**

 Each participant was tested in only one condition (noise or no noise.

 There were two separate (independent) groups of participants.

We could redesign this as a **repeated measures design**.

 Each participant would be tested in both conditions. They would be tested in the noise condition and retested in the no noise condition.

	Noise condition			No noise condition		
Independent groups	Sara	Rob	Mike	Linda	Pip	Janet
	Paul	Sue	Sam	Chris	Rosie	Jack
Repeated measures	Sara	Rob	Mike	Sara	Rob	Mike
	Paul	Sue	Sam	Paul	Sue	Sam

Repeated measures
Same participants in each condition (noise or no noise).

Independent groups
Two (or more) groups of participants, one for each condition.

These are called **experimental designs.**

The experiment on the Stroop effect was an example of a **repeated measures design**.

Each participant was tested on both conditions (i.e. variations of the IV) – words that were either conflicting or not conflicting.

Learning about research methods is a bit like learning a foreign language. When you learn a foreign language, you have to learn a new set of words and more especially what they mean. One of the best ways to do this is to speak the language – the same is true for research methods. Don't hold back, start using the words.

Qs
6

Noise and memory

1. Write a suitable hypothesis for the new version of the experiment that uses a repeated measures design.

2. Explain why you think that the repeated measures design would not be as good as the independent groups design.

Stroop effect

3. How could you do this study as an independent groups design?

4. What might be the disadvantage of using an independent groups design for this experiment?

Alcohol and goldfish

5. Was this an independent groups design or a repeated measures design?

Is performance affected by expectation?

6. Was this an independent groups design or a repeated measures design?

7. What do you think was the advantage of choosing this design?

For each of the following experiments, state whether it is a repeated measures or an independent groups design.

To do this, ask yourself, 'Would the findings be analysed by comparing the scores from the same person or by comparing the scores of two (or more) groups of people?' (Write your answer down.)

8. Boys and girls are compared on their IQ test scores.

9. Hamsters are tested to see if one genetic strain is better at finding food in a maze than another group.

10. Reaction time is tested before and after a reaction time training activity to see if test scores improve after training.

11. Participants are tested on a memory task in the morning and in the afternoon.

12. Three groups of participants are each asked to remember different word lists (one with nouns, one with verbs and one with adjectives) to see which is easier to recall.

13. Participants are asked to give ratings for attractive and unattractive photographs.

Try this one

In Stroop's original study, the participants had two word lists: one of colour words in a conflicting colour, the other was of colour words printed in black. There were two groups of participants:

- Group 1 read conflicting colour and then black words.

- Group 2 read black and then conflicting colour words.

This was done to control for practice and fatigue (called **order effects**, as you will see on the next page).

Is this now an independent groups design, or is it still a repeated measures?

It is still repeated measures because the analysis still involves comparing the same individual's performance on two conditions (conflicting colour and black words).

Repeated measures

Disadvantages

1. One of the memory tests may be more difficult than the other and this is why the participants do better in one condition (the noise condition) than the other (no noise condition).

2. When the participants do the second memory test, they may guess the purpose of the experiment, which may affect their behaviour. For example, some participants may purposely do worse on the second test because they want it to seem as if they work better in noisy conditions.

3. The order of the conditions may affect performance (an **order effect**). Participants may do better on the second test because of a **practice effect** OR participants may do worse on the second test because of being bored with doing the same test again (**boredom** or **fatigue effect**).

Advantages

You can work out the advantages by looking at the disadvantages of independent groups design.

Dealing with the problems created by repeated measures design

Dealing with point 1.

You can make sure the tests are equivalent. Create a list of 40 words and **randomly allocate** these to two lists so both lists are equivalent.

Dealing with point 2.

You can lie to the participants about the purpose of the test to try to prevent them guessing what it is about. This is called a **single blind** design (the participant is blind to the aim of the study).

Dealing with point 3.

You can use **counterbalancing** (see right).

Independent groups

Disadvantages

- No control of **participant variables** (i.e. the different abilities of each participant). For example, participants in Group 1 might be more able than those in Group 2.
- You need twice as many participants.

Advantages

You can work out the advantages by looking at the disadvantages of repeated measures design.

Dealing with the problems created by independent groups design

1. Randomly allocate participants to conditions to ensure that the groups are equivalent (see 'randomness' on page 12).

2. Match participants in each group on key variables (see below).

Matched participants design

This is a third kind of experimental design. It involves the use of independent groups, but each participant in Group A is paired with one in Group B. This is done by pairing participants on key variables (e.g. IQ, memory ability, gender – any characteristic that might affect the findings) and then placing one member of each pair into each group.

Disadvantages

- Very time-consuming to match the participants.
- May not control all the participant variables.

Advantages

- Controls some participant variables.
- Participants are less likely to guess study's aims.

Counterbalancing

Counterbalancing ensures that each condition is tested first or second in equal amounts, as we did for the Stroop effect (see page 7). If participants read a conflicting list first and then a non-conflicting list, we might expect them to read the second list more quickly because they had had more practice.

There are two ways to counterbalance order effects:

Way 1. Counterbalancing

Group 1: the participants do the conflicting list first and then the non-conflicting words.

Group 2: participants do the non-conflicting list first and then the conflicting list.

This is still a repeated measures design even though there are two groups of participants because a comparison will be made for each participant on their performance on the two conditions (conflict and no conflict).

Way 2. ABBA

Condition A: conflicting lists.

Condition B: non-conflicting list.

Each participant takes part in every trial.

Trial 1: Conflicting list (A)

Trial 2: Non-conflicting list (B)

Trial 3: Non-conflicting list (B)

Trial 4: Conflicting list A

Counterbalancing literally means achieving balance by having an equal weight at both ends.

Qs 7

1. Which of the two forms of counterbalancing (1 or 2) did we use in the experiment on the Stroop effect on page 7?

2. What participant variables might have affected the findings of the Stroop effect study?

3. To what extent were these participant variables controlled?

4. Look back to the experiment 'Is performance affected by expectation?' on page 6. Counterbalancing has been used here, although not for order effects. Explain in what way this design is counterbalanced.

5. *A psychologist conducted a study to see whether visual imagery helps memory. To do this, there were two lists to be recalled – one had words only, the other had images instead of words.*

   a. Describe how you could conduct this study using (a) a repeated measures design, (b) an independent groups design and (c) a matched pairs design.

   b. Which design would be best? Explain your answer.

   c. For which kind of design would counterbalancing be necessary?

   d. Explain how you would design the counterbalancing.

KEY TERMS

Counterbalancing
Matched participants design
Order effect
Participant variable
Random allocation
Single blind

Selection of participants

When conducting any research study you need to find some participants!

Participants are drawn from **'the target population'**: the group of people that the researcher is interested in.

This is a selection or **sample** of the target population.

Researchers make generalisations about the target population from the sample as long as the sample is *representative of the target population* (i.e. represents the target population).

*All sampling methods aim to produce a **representative** sample but are inevitably **biased**.*

Opportunity sample

How? Ask people walking by you in the street, i.e. select those who are available.

☺ The easiest method because you just use the first participants you can find.

☹ Inevitably biased because the sample is drawn from a small part of the target population. For example, if you do an experiment using people in the street, the sample is selected from people walking around the centre of a town – not those who work, or those living in rural areas.

Volunteer sample

How? Advertise in a newspaper or on a noticeboard.

☺ Access to a variety of participants.

☹ The sample is biased because the participants are likely to be more highly motivated and/or have extra time on their hands (= **volunteer bias**).

Random sample

How? Put the names of the target population into a hat and draw out the required number.

☺ Unbiased: all members of the target population have an equal chance of selection.

☹ You usually end up with a biased sample (e.g. more boys than girls) because the sample is usually too small (see Activity 3).

A sampling method is about how participants are identified NOT about who eventually takes part. For example, in an opportunity or random sample, some potential participants may refuse to take part. The remaining participants are 'volunteers'.

This is not true for all opportunity/random samples as in a field experiment described in chapter 2, where participants cannot refuse.

Quota sample

How? Subgroups within a population are identified (e.g. boys and girls or age groups: 10-12, 13-14 etc.). Then an opportunity sample (quota) is taken from each subgroup

☺ More representative than an opportunity sample because equal representation of subgroups.

☹ Although the sample represents the subgroups, each quota taken may be biased in other ways.

Systematic sample

How? Selecting every nth person from a list of the target population.

☺ Sample is spread evenly across the population, avoiding bias.

☹ The sample may be unrepresentative if the systematic basis does not allow for all subgroups within the population to be captured e.g. if every 10th person is always sitting at the front of the class.

Randomness

The most obvious way to obtain a random selection is to draw numbers or names *'out of a hat'*. It is sometimes called the 'lottery method'.

Random selection is used to obtain a **random sample** of participants (as described above) or for the **random allocation** of participants to conditions when using an independent measures design (as described on the previous page). For random allocation, for example, you put all the participants' names into a hat and draw out half of the names for group 1 and place the remaining names in group 2.

Many students mistake a **systematic sample** for a random sample – selecting every 10th person is not random, it is a systematic method of selection. However, if you select a number using a random method and start with this person and then you select every 10th person, this would be a random sample.

If you want equal numbers of girls and boys (or 10 and 11th years, etc.), one way to do this is to put all the boys' names in a hat and draw out 5, and do the same for the girls' names. This is called a **stratified samp**

Activity 3

Take 40 pieces of paper and write 20 boys' names and 20 girls' names.

Put them in a hat and draw out 10 slips of paper. If the selection is unbiased, you should ideally get five boys and five girls.

Put the slips of paper back and draw 10 out again. Repeat this a total of four times and then try it with a larger sample (20). Each time, record how many boys' and girls' names were drawn. You can record your results in the table below.

	Sample size 10				Sample size 20				Total
Trial no:	1	2	3	4	1	2	3	4	
Boys									
Girls									

The point is that, in principle, random selection results in an unbiased and representative sample, but only if the sample is large enough.

Is this what you found? What happens if you put 40 boys' names and 40 girls' names in the hat?

KEY TERMS

Advantages ☺ and disadvantages ☹, and how to do:

Operationalisation
Opportunity sample
Quota sample
Random sample
Selection of participants

***Random** means that each member of the population has an equal chance of being selected.*

Operationalisation

Qs **8**

1. Look back to page 9, Question 5. You were asked to write a hypothesis for three studies. Now write an aim and a research prediction for each of these three studies.

2. *A psychologist conducted a study to look at whether watching certain films made children more helpful (one film was about being helpful, the other was neutral). He advertised for participants in the local newspaper. A large number of children volunteered, and a sample of 30 was selected for the actual experiment.*

   a. What is the IV in this experiment?

   b. What is the DV?

   c. How could you operationalise the DV?

   d. State a suitable hypothesis and/or research prediction for this study.

   e. Is your prediction directional or non-directional?

   f. Explain your choice of direction.

   g. What kind of experimental design would you use in this study?

   h. Describe **one** disadvantage of this experimental design.

   i. How could you deal with this problem?

   j. Describe the target population.

   k. What kind of sample was obtained?

   l. Suggest how the experimenter might select the sub-sample from all those who applied.

3. *A psychology experiment aims to investigate how preschool children differ from those already at school in terms of their ability to remember symbols that look like letters.*

   a. If the experimenter wanted to obtain a random sample of each of the two age groups, how might this have been done?

   b. Explain the purpose of using a random sample.

   c. What is the IV in the experiment?

   d. What is the DV?

   e. The children were shown 20 different symbols. Why was it better to use 20 symbols rather than just two?

   f. Why might it be better to use two rather than 20 symbols?

4. *Mary Smith organises a project to enable her psychology class to have a go at using a matched participants design. The class is divided into two groups; one will receive word list A (nouns) and the other word list B (verbs). They will be tested on recall.*

   a. Suggest **two** participant variables that could be used to match the classmates.

   b. Explain why each of the variables you chose would be important to control in this study.

   c. What are the two conditions in the experiment?

   d. If Mary had decided to use an independent measures design, suggest **two** ways in which participants could have been allocated to the conditions.

   e. Mary used words that were all of two syllables and of similar length. Give **one** reason why.

   f. Mary decided to repeat the study using all the pupils in the school. She selected every fifth pupil on the register. Why is this not a random sample?

A 'good' hypothesis should be written in a testable form, i.e. in a way that makes it clear how you are going to design an experiment to test the hypothesis.

Think back to the Stroop effect. Stroop's research aim was to investigate the effects of interference on performance speeds. To turn this aim into an experiment, he needed to state his belief:

Hypothesis *People take longer to perform a task when word and colour conflict with each other than when they do not.*

The concept of 'interference' has been **operationalised** in order to produce a testable hypothesis ('interference' = 'word and colour conflict'). 'Operationalisation' means specifying a set of operations or behaviours that can be measured or manipulated. For example:

Hypothesis *People work better in quiet rather than noisy conditions.*

What precisely do we mean by 'work better' and 'quiet' and 'noisy'? We need to define the operations:

'work better' = obtain a higher score on a memory test
'quiet' = no sound
'noisy' = radio playing.

Operationalised hypothesis *People obtain a higher score on a memory test when tested in quiet (no sounds) rather than noisy (radio playing) conditions.*

Hypothesis *People are happier if they work.*

'happier' = higher score on happiness questionnaire
'work'   = have a full-time job (over 40 hours per week).

Operationalised hypothesis *People obtain a higher score on a happiness questionnaire if they work full time (over 40 hours per week) than if they work part time (less than 20 hours per week).*

> Don't make the mistake of confusing the terms hypothesis and research prediction. There is an important difference. A hypothesis is a general claim about the world. In order to test a hypothesis, we need a prediction about how the participants in a study will behave.
>
> The **hypothesis** is about **populations** (people). It states our expectation about the world. It can be operationalised.
>
> The **research prediction** is about **samples** (participants). It predicts what we expect to find in a study. It is stated in the future tense and must be operationalised.

Qs **9**

1. Do older people sleep more or less than younger people?

   a. Identify the IV and DV in this experiment.

   b. How could you operationalise the IV and DV?

   c. Write a fully operationalised directional hypothesis.

   d. Write a fully operationalised non-directional hypothesis.

2. *People rate food as looking more attractive when they are hungry.* Answer questions a–d above.

3. *A teacher wishes to find out whether one maths test is harder than another maths test.* Answer questions a–d above.

Experimental control

There are DVs and IVs, and then there are extraneous variables . . .

The experimenter 'controls' the IV in an experiment – making it change to see what happens. The experimenter also has to control other variables (**extraneous variables**) to make sure they do not change – otherwise this may spoil the experiment.

Order effects are an **extraneous variable**.

For example, in the noise and memory experiment (*repeated measures design*), noise (IV) should affect recall (DV).

1. Participants do the memory test with noise.

2. Participants do the memory test without noise.

They do better on the second test.

Is this because they do better when tested without noise? (Noise/no noise is the IV.)

Or because they have *practised* doing the test? (Practice/no practice has become an alternative and unintentional IV.)

Practice/no practice is an extraneous variable.

*An **extraneous variable** is a variable other than the IV that may affect the DV and should thus be controlled. The term is used interchangeably with the term **uncontrolled variable**.*

*A **confounding variable** is a variable other than the IV that has affected the DV and has thus confounded the findings of the study.*

another extraneous variable . . .

Noise and memory experiment (*independent groups design*)

Group 1 does the test with noise in the morning.

Group 2 does the test without noise in the afternoon.

Group 2 does better on the test.

Is this because people do better when tested without noise? (Noise/no noise is the IV.)

Or because people do better on memory tests when tested in the afternoon?

Time of day has become a substitute IV – it is an extraneous variable.

Qs   **10**

1. In the repeated measures study described above, how could you control the extraneous variable?

2. In the independent groups study described on the right, how could you control the extraneous variable?

---

still more extraneous variables . . .

Consider the Stroop effect study. Imagine that each participant is tested individually. In this situation, there may be both **situational** and **participant extraneous variables**.

• Some participants are tested in a noisy classroom, whereas others are tested in a quiet one-to-one situation.

• One participant is wearing tinted glasses.

• Some participants are uncertain so the experimenter offers to help them fill in the answer sheet.

• In later test sessions the sun is setting and making the test room glow orange.

All of these variations may affect participant performance and may affect the DV.

*Standardised procedures include **standardised instructions** – the instructions given to participants about what to do.*

and a final extraneous variable . . .

Finally, we can consider **investigator effects.** The behaviour of an investigator/experimenter may affect the participants and thus affect the DV.

For example, the way in which the investigator asks a question may *lead* the participant to give the answer the investigator 'wants'.

Or the way in which the investigator responds may encourage certain kinds of response. For example, the investigator may smile as if to say, 'Yes, that's the right answer'.

How to deal with this extraneous variable

Experimenters use **standardised procedures** to ensure that all participants receive the same instructions and to prevent the experimenter affecting participants' behaviour, for example by using leading questions.

Standardised procedures are like a recipe – if different procedures are used, the different outcomes may be due to the procedures and not the IV.

How to deal with investigator effects

Investigators use **standardised instructions** to prevent using leading questions.

Or you can use a **double blind** design – neither the participant nor the person conducting the experiment (who has not designed it) knows the aims of the experiment; therefore, the experimenter cannot affect the participants' performance.

The way in which an investigator asks a question (the words used, the tone of voice, the facial expression) may affect the responses that are given.

KEY TERMS

Confederate
Control
Confounding variable
Debriefing
Extraneous variable
Investigator effects
Standardised procedures

Confederates

The IV in an experiment is sometimes a person.

Core Study

For example, one of the IVs in the study by Schachter and Singer (1962) on emotion involved a confederate.

Schachter and Singer thought that emotion resulted from (i) physiological arousal plus (ii) labelling the arousal as an emotion on the basis of how we interpret the situation we are in. To test this, they needed to manipulate the situation participants were in, after they had been given an injection of adrenaline (epinephrine) without their knowledge. Some participants were put in a euphoric (very happy) condition; others were put in an *angry* condition.

This was achieved by the use of **confederates** (also called 'stooges'), pretending to be another participant waiting. The euphoric confederate would play paper aeroplanes, paper basketball and hula hoop whilst waiting! The angry confederate got increasingly angry over a questionnaire and ended up ripping it up into pieces and throwing it on the floor. Some of the participants did interpret their physiological arousal in terms of the context i.e. the emotion conveyed by the confederate.

Thus, the confederate provided one of the IVs. But there are always ethical problems with this procedure. See right.

Confederates are individuals in an experiment who are not real participants and have been instructed how to behave by the experimenter.

Would this man make you feel happy? Perhaps if you were physiologically aroused (rapid heart beat, sweating and trembling) you might think your state of arousal was actually happiness.

Ethics

In your study of psychology, you will be aware of ethical criticisms. Many studies are criticised for lack of ethics. It is not acceptable for participants to be harmed during the course of any experiment.

What, however, constitutes 'harm'? Is it harmful for a person to experience mild discomfort or mild stress?

Is it acceptable to lie to participants about what an experiment is about? Such deception may be necessary so that participants' behaviour is not affected by knowing the aim of the experiment.

One way to deal with deception is to **debrief** participants afterwards. At the start of an experiment, participants are briefed about what the task will involve. At the end, they are debriefed. This debriefing has two functions:

1. *Ethical*: It is an opportunity to reassure the participant about their performance. If any deception took place, participants are told the true aims of the study and offered the opportunity to discuss any concerns they may have. They may be offered the opportunity to withhold their data from the study.

2. *Practical*: The debrief allows the researcher to thank individuals for participating. The experimenter may ask for further information about the research topic. For example, he or she may ask why the participant found one condition more difficult, or may ask whether the participant believed the set-up.

Briefing for an experiment

This experiment is concerned with reading coloured print. Some people find it harder to identify certain colours. You will be shown five word lists and asked to identify the colours of the written words.

Qs   11

1. Who was the confederate in Milgram's study of obedience (if you are not familiar with this study, see outline on page 27)?
2. Why do you need to 'brief' participants?
3. Why is it necessary to debrief participants?
4. Why would it be necessary to deceive participants in the study described on the left?
5. Imagine you were given the briefing and debriefing shown here. What answers would you give to Questions 3 and 4?

Debriefing

Thank you for taking part in the experiment. The true purpose of the study was to find out if it takes longer to identify the word colour when the word and colour are conflicting. This is called the Stroop effect.

1. Would you like to know the overall findings from the study?   YES/NO

2. Did you feel distressed by any aspect of the study?   YES/NO

3. What did you think the purpose of the study was?

4. Did you think that some of the lists were harder to read than others?   YES/NO
If yes, which lists?

5. Do you think this might have affected your performance?   YES/NO
If yes, in what way?

DIY Design it yourself

Two possible activities are suggested on this page. They enable you to try to design and conduct your own experiment. Questions 12 will guide you in designing and conducting your experiment.

Activity 4 — Memory and organisation

A favourite experiment for students is one that concerns organisation and memory. If words are presented to a participant in categories (as shown on the near right), they are more easily memorised than if they are presented in a random order (list on the far right).

Qs 12

Design decisions to make – answer these questions for either Activity 4 or Activity 5 (whether or not you are actually doing the activities).

1. What is the IV and what is the DV?
2. How should the IV be operationalised?
3. How will the DV be operationalised (i.e. how will you measure it?)?
4. Should you use repeated measures or independent groups? Write down the relative advantages/disadvantages of each.
5. Write a suitable aim and hypothesis for your study and a research prediction.
6. How many participants will you need?
7. How will you select these participants? (For ethical reasons, you should only use participants over the age of 16.)
8. Are there any extraneous (situational or participant) variables that need to be controlled?
9. How will you control these?
10. Are there any investigator effects to control?
11. How can you control these?
12. Write your standardised procedure, including a briefing and a debriefing.
    NOW conduct a pilot study and make any alterations to the design that are necessary.
13. After you have conducted the study, record the findings for each participant in a table.
    If you do not have time to conduct this experiment yourself, invent an appropriate set of data.
14. What do you conclude from your findings?
15. Identify **one** problem you discovered when conducting this study.

*A **conclusion** is the statement(s) you make about human behaviour (populations) on the basis of your research study with a small set of participants (a sample). Conclusions should be written in the present tense and be about 'people' rather than 'participants'.*

Activity 5 — Emotion

One theory of emotion proposes that we experience general levels of physiological arousal and label these as love, attraction, fear, stress, etc. according to the cues that are available.

For example, if you are physiologically aroused (e.g. from watching a scary movie) and at the same time are in the presence of an attractive man or woman, you might feel the arousal is because that person is attractive to you.

One experiment that tested this arranged for participants to run on the spot for one minute (creating physiological arousal) and then rate a set of photographs for attractiveness. Those people who did not run on the spot gave lower ratings than those who did (White et al., 1981).

Does this photograph look more attractive to someone who has been running on the spot for a minute?

You might describe your findings using the methods outlined on page 17.

Organised list	Random list
Dogs	Pear
Labrador	Beagle
Beagle	Clarinet
Boxer	Hail
Spaniel	Rain
Fruit	Drinks
Apple	Rose
Pear	Squash
Plum	Hand
Orange	Boxer
Weather	Iron
Snow	Coke
Rain	Gold
Sleet	Harp
Hail	Piano
Flowers	Metal
Daffodil	Apple
Rose	Body
Pansy	Fruit
Tulip	Instruments
Instruments	Daffodil
Harp	Plum
Piano	Nose
Flute	Weather
Clarinet	Copper
Drinks	Labrador
Water	Water
Milk	Flowers
Squash	Brass
Coke	Foot
Body	Tulips
Nose	Pansy
Foot	Dogs
Toe	Sleet
Hand	Milk
Metal	Orange
Brass	Toe
Gold	Snow
Copper	Flute
Iron	Spaniel

KEY TERMS

Bar chart
Mean
Measures of central tendency
Measures of dispersion
Median
Mode
Pie chart
Range

Descriptive statistics: How to represent your data

*There are three ways to **describe** the data that you found from your research.*

Measures of central tendency

Measures of central tendency inform us about central (or middle) values of a set of data. There are three different 'averages' – ways of calculating a typical value for a set of data.

The **mean** is calculated by adding up all the numbers and dividing by the number of numbers.

☺ It makes use of the *values* of all the data.

☹ It can be misrepresentative of the numbers if there is an extreme value.

☹ It can only be used with **interval** or **ratio** data.

The **median** is the *middle* value in an *ordered* list.

☺ It is not affected by extreme scores.

☺ It can be used with **ordinal data**.

☹ It is not as 'sensitive' as the mean because not all values are reflected in the median.

The **mode** is the value that is *most* common.

☺ It is useful when the data are in categories (such as number of people who like pink), i.e. **nominal data**.

☹ It is not a useful way of describing data when there are several modes.

Measures of dispersion

A set of data can also be described in terms of how dispersed, or spread out, the numbers are.

The easiest way to do this is to use the **range**. Consider the data sets below:

3, 5, 8, 8, 9, 10, 12, 12, 13, 15

mean = 9.5   range = 12 (3 to 15)

1, 5, 8, 8, 9, 10, 12, 12, 13, 17

mean = 9.5   range = 16 (1 to 17)

The two sets of numbers have the same mean but a different range, so the range is helpful as a further method of describing the data. If we just used the mean, the data would appear to be the same.

The **range** is the difference between the highest and lowest numbers.

☺ Provides you with direct information

☺ Easy to calculate

☹ Affected by extreme values

☹ Does not take into account the number of observations in the data set

Levels of measurement (nominal, ordinal, interval and ratio) are explained on page 137.

Visual display

A picture is worth a thousand words! Graphs provide a means of 'eyeballing' your data and seeing the findings at a glance.

Bar chart: The height of the bar represents frequency. Unlike a histogram, you can exclude empty categories. There is no true zero, and data on the horizontal axis are not continuous. Suitable for words and numbers.

Pie charts: A circle that is divided into slices where the angle of the slice represents the frequency of each item. For example, if people were asked to name their favourite football team and 20% choose Manchester United, 35% choose Chelsea and 45% choose Liverpool then you can calculate the angle of the slice by working out 20%, 35%, and 45% of 360 degrees in a circle.

See next page for more on graphs.

Special tip

CENTRAL TENDENCY	MEAN MEDIAN MODE

Many candidates find it hard to remember the link between 'measures of central tendency' and 'mean, median, mode'.

One way to help you remember links is to produce memorable pictures. The flag above is an attempt to illustrate the idea of a central tendency and link this to the three appropriate terms. Try to develop your own memorable picture for this and other concepts – the more outrageous, the better!

Qs 13

1. For each of the data sets below, calculate the (a) mean, (b) median and (c) mode, (d) state which of these would be most suitable to use and why.

	Data set
1.	2, 3, 5, 6, 6, 8, 9, 12, 15, 21, 22
2.	2, 3, 8, 10, 11, 13, 13, 14, 14, 29
3.	2, 2, 4, 5, 5, 5, 7, 7, 8, 8, 8, 10
4.	cat, cat, dog, budgie, snake, gerbil

2. Why is it better to know about the mean and range of a data set rather than just the mean?

3. A class of psychology students studies the Stroop effect and produces the following data showing the time taken (in seconds) to read each kind of word list:

Student	1	2	3	4	5	6	7	8	9	10	11	12
Colour conflict	29	25	20	26	22	31	28	28	26	28	21	29
No conflict	20	16	14	20	18	21	20	17	20	19	15	16

(a) What measure of central tendency would be most suitable to use to describe this data? Explain your answer.

(b) Draw both a bar chart and a pie chart to represent the data from this study.

More on graphs

A graph should be simple. It should clearly show the findings from a study.

There should be a short title.

The x axis must be labelled (the x axis goes across the page; it is usually the IV).

The y axis must be labelled (the y axis goes up vertically; it is usually the DV or 'frequency').

Always use squared paper if you are hand-drawing graphs.

Aims, procedures, findings and conclusions

When psychologists conduct research, they write a report of their study that contains the following information: **aims** (the intended area of study), **procedures** (a description of the **standardised procedures** so that the study can be repeated), **findings** (the data or results produced by the study) and **conclusions** (an interpretation of the findings).

This is an example of a finding:

Participants obtained a higher score when tested in the no noise condition.

This is an example of a conclusion:

The findings suggest that people work better on memory tasks when there is little noise.

The distinction is subtle but important. One is a fact about the *participants*, the other is a generalisation made about what *people* do. Like the distinction between a hypothesis and a research prediction, findings are about *samples*, conclusions are about *populations*.

Qs 14

1. Why is Graph A meaningless?
2. Write a title that would be suitable for all three graphs.
3. Describe the y axis of all three graphs.
4. A class of psychology students studies the Stroop effect and produces the following data showing the time taken (in seconds) to read each kind of word list:

Student	1	2	3	4	5	6	7	8	9	10	11	12
Colour conflict	29	25	20	26	22	31	28	28	26	28	21	29
No conflict	20	16	14	20	18	21	20	17	20	19	15	16

  a. Calculate the mean, median, mode and range for each data set.
  b. What measure of central tendency would be most suitable to use to describe this data?
  c. Draw a bar chart to represent the data from this study.

Each of the graphs below presents the data collected in an experiment on organisation and memory.

Only one of these graphs is useful; two of them are a 'waste of time' – which one is the useful one?

Graph A

Participant number 1 in the organised word group is placed next to participant number 1 in the random word group. Students like to draw 'participant charts' BUT THEY ARE TOTALLY MEANINGLESS.

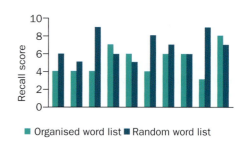

■ Organised word list ■ Random word list

Graph B

The findings from each participant are shown in this graph. They are grouped together so that you can see all the scores from participants in the organised word group and all the scores from the participants in the random word group.

This is *slightly better* than Graph A because we can just about tell that the random word list led to better recall – but a glance at the means (as in Graph C) shows this effortlessly.

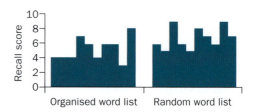

Graph C

This graph shows the mean scores for each group. The findings are clear, which is the point of using a graph.

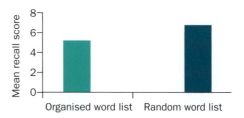

Note: *the horizontal axis of a graph is called the x axis, and the vertical axis is called the y axis.*

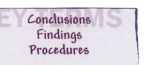

KEY TERMS
Conclusions
Findings
Procedures

Multiple choice questions

1. The independent variable in a study is
   a. The one that is excluded.
   b. The one that is manipulated by the experimenter.
   c. The one that is observed or measured.
   d. Not of interest to the experimenter.

2. A pilot study is
   a. The first study conducted by a research team.
   b. A preliminary investigation.
   c. A small-scale trial run of a research design.
   d. A research project on efficient flying of aeroplanes.

3. Which of the following hypotheses is a non-directional hypothesis?
   a. Participants in the no noise condition do better on the memory test than those in the noise condition.
   b. Participants who drink alcohol have a slower reaction time than those who have no alcohol.
   c. Participants like words that are familiar more than those that are not familiar.
   d. Participants who expect to perform better perform differently from those given lower expectations.

4. One reason for using a directional hypothesis is because
   a. Past research suggests that participants will do better on one condition than another.
   b. Past research is uncertain about how participants will perform.
   c. There is no past research.
   d. The researcher wants to make a strong statement.

5. An extraneous variable is a variable that
   a. Has been controlled by the experimenter.
   b. Confounds the findings of the study.
   c. May influence the dependent variable.
   d. The experimenter wants to find out more about.

6. A student plans to investigate the effects of practice on IQ test performance. Some participants are given two practice tests prior to the IQ test, whereas others do no test beforehand. The dependent variable in this study is
   a. The participants.
   b. The effects of practice.
   c. The IQ test performance before the study.
   d. The IQ test performance at the end of the study.

7. The study described in question 6 is
   a. A repeated measures design.
   b. An independent groups design.
   c. A matched pairs design.
   d. A careful design.

8. In an independent groups design
   a. There are two or more separate groups of participants.
   b. The analysis involves comparing measures from two or more separate groups of people.
   c. The analysis involves comparing two measures from the same person.
   d. Both a and b.

9. One advantage of doing a matched participant design is
   a. You need fewer participants than for repeated measures.
   b. You can control some participant variables.
   c. Order effects are not a problem.
   d. Both b and c.

10. The letters 'ABBA' refer to a research design
    a. Created by a Swedish rock band.
    b. To control participant variables.
    c. To counterbalance for order effects.
    d. To control extraneous variables.

11. All sampling methods are
    a. Representative of the target population.
    b. Biased.
    c. Random.
    d. Difficult to conduct.

12. Selecting participants who just happen to be available is called
    a. Opportunity sampling.
    b. Volunteer sampling.
    c. Random sampling.
    d. Quota sampling.

13. Which of the following could not be an extraneous variable in a study
    a. An investigator effect.
    b. A confederate.
    c. An order effect.
    d. A lack of standardised procedures.

14. One way to improve the design of a study is to:
    a. Conduct a pilot study beforehand to see if some things do not work.
    b. Have lots of variables.
    c. Use a repeated measures design.
    d. Use a confederate.

15. Which of the following is a disadvantage of using a repeated measures design?
    a. It does not control participant variables.
    b. You have to use more participants than for an independent groups design.
    c. There are more likely to be investigator effects than for an independent groups design.
    d. There may be order effects.

16. In an experiment, half the participants do Condition A first followed by Condition B, whereas the other participants do the conditions in the reverse order. This procedure is called
    a. Countercontrol.
    b. Countercalling.
    c. Counterbalancing.
    d. Counteracting.

17. An individual who is instructed about how to behave by the researcher, often acting as the IV, is called
    a. An extraneous variable.
    b. A dependent variable.
    c. The investigator.
    d. A confederate.

18. Which of the following is a random sample?
    a. Names drawn from a hat.
    b. Asking people if they would like to take part.
    c. Using every 10th name on a register.
    d. Taking whoever happens to be there.

19. Which of the following is a measure of central tendency?
    a. Range.
    b. Bar chart.
    c. Mode.
    d. Interval.

20. Debriefing involves
    a. Telling a participant the true aims of a study.
    b. Giving participants a chance to discuss any psychological harm they may have experienced.
    c. Asking participants for feedback about the experiment.
    d. All of the above.

Contents

More about experiments

field experiments and natural experiments

Field experiments

In Chapter 1, we considered experiments. All experiments have an independent variable and a dependent variable.

There are different kinds of experiment:

Laboratory experiment
An experiment conducted in a *special environment* where variables can be *carefully controlled*. Participants are aware that they are taking part in an experiment, although they may not know the true aims of the study.

Field experiment
An experiment conducted in a more *natural environment*, i.e. 'in the field'. As with the laboratory experiment, the independent variable is still *deliberately manipulated* by the researcher. Participants are *often not aware* that they are participating in an experiment.

Field study
Any study that is conducted in a natural environment. Note that not all studies conducted in a laboratory are experiments. There are controlled observations that are conducted in a laboratory (which we will look at in Chapter 4).

Core Study

A field experiment: The subway Samaritan

Helping behaviour was investigated in a study on the New York subway by Piliavin, Rodin and Piliavin (1969). The aim of the study was to investigate what things made people more or less willing to help someone in an emergency situation.

To investigate this, the study involved a staged emergency – several observers boarded a subway train and then a confederate collapsed in the subway carriage. There were two conditions used to see whether people who are responsible for their own plight receive less help'.

- *The 'drunk' condition:* The victim smells of alcohol and carries a bottle wrapped in a brown paper bag (as they do in New York).

- *The cane condition:* The victim appears sober and carries a cane.

Seventy seconds after the train pulled out of the station, the male victim (a confederate) staggers and collapses. The observers recorded how long it took for help to be forthcoming, as well as information about the race, gender, and location of all the passengers in the compartment and of all those who offered help. The observers also noted any comments overheard as well as eliciting comments from people sitting nearby.

Piliavin *et al.* found that when the victim carried a cane 95% of bystanders helped within 10 seconds; if he appeared drunk help only came in 50% of the trials. Furthermore, the cane victim was helped on average within 5 seconds whereas the drunk victim was helped after 109 seconds.

An experiment permits us to study **cause and effect.** It differs from non-experimental methods in that it involves the manipulation of one variable (the independent variable – IV), while trying to keep all other variables constant. If the IV is the only thing that is changed, then it must be responsible for any change in the dependent variable (DV).

Qs 15

1. What are the research aims of the experiment on the left?

2. How do you know it is an experiment?

3. How do you know it is a field experiment?

4. Write a suitable hypothesis for this experiment.

5. Why should the victim be played by the same person in each of the two conditions (instead of using two confederates)?

6. What is a 'confederate'?

7. What sampling method was used to select your participants?

8. Give **one** advantage and **one** disadvantage of using this method of selecting participants.

9. Do you feel the participants were a reasonably representative sample of the general population? Why or why not?

10. What was the experimental design that was used?

11. Can you think of **one** ethical issue raised in this study (i.e. something that may harm participants)?

12. Present the results in a table like the one below.

	Drunk condition	Cane condition
Frequency of helping		
Average time taken for help to be offered		

13. Draw a graph to illustrate these results.

14. What do you conclude?

Lab versus field experiments

It may help you to understand the difference between lab and field experiments by looking at the examples on this page.

A Helping behaviour was investigated in a suburban street. A confederate got out of a car and dropped some books as a pedestrian approached. The confederate was either in a 'low need' condition (able bodied) or in a 'high need' condition (with arm in a cast). Background noise was varied by either having a lawnmower going (87dB) or not. Matthews and Cannon (1975) found that the stooge received help most frequently when wearing the arm cast (80% of the time) but that this was dramatically reduced in the noisy lawnmower condition to just 20%.

B Leventhal et al. (1967) wanted to investigate how to get people to stop smoking. Smokers were invited to the university and either shown a demonstration of smoke entering a mechanical 'smoking machine'; or they were shown a short, fear-arousing, film of an operation on the lungs of a diseased smoker (so disturbing a number of participants walked out). Afterwards, both groups were asked about their intention to stop smoking. Smokers in the fear arousal condition were much more likely to say they intended to give up.

C The participants were children aged 3–5 years old. Each child was taken on their own to a special room where there were lots of toys including, in one corner, a 5-foot inflatable Bobo doll and a mallet. The experimenter invited the 'model' to join them and then left the room for about 10 minutes. Half of the children watched the model playing aggressively with a life-sized Bobo doll while the others watched the model play non-aggressively with the doll. Later they were given an opportunity to play with toys, including the Bobo doll, and were observed through a one-way mirror. The children who saw the aggressive behaviour were more likely to behave aggressively (Bandura et al., 1961; see right).

D One group of school pupils were given information about how their peers had performed on a maths task. They were either told that their peers had done well or that they had done poorly on the test. The children were later given a maths test in class. Those who expected to do well did better than those led to expect they would do poorly (Schunk, 1983).

E The Hawthorne Electric factory in Chicago asked researchers to study what factors led to increased worker productivity. The study found that increased lighting led to increased productivity – but then also found that decreased lighting led to increased activity (Roethlisberger and Dickson, 1939).

The conclusion was that the participants knew they were being studied and this interest in their work was what explained their increased output, masking the real IV. This has been called the **Hawthorne effect**.

F To investigate eye-witness memory, students were shown a video of a car crash and asked a number of questions afterwards. The key question was 'how fast was the car going when it ____?'. The IV was whether the word was "smashed", "hit", "contacted". A week later, participants were asked 'did you see any broken glass?'. Participants who had been asked the "smashed" question were twice as likely to say they had had seen glass, even though there was none. Loftus and Palmer (1974) concluded that the questions had interfered with the participants' memory of the event seen on video.

Lab experiments are artificial or 'contrived'

- Participants know they are being studied, and this is likely to affect their behaviour.
- The setting is often not like real life. This is described as being low in **mundane realism**. People behave more like they 'normally' do when a study is high in mundane realism.
- The IV or DV may be operationalised in such a way that it does not represent real-life experiences, e.g. using trigrams to test how memory works.

For all these reasons, participants in a laboratory experiment are less likely to behave as they would in real life.

The same problems may also arise in field experiments; so that field experiments are not necessarily more like real life then laboratory experiments.

Mundane realism refers to how an experiment mirrors the real world. 'Mundane' means 'of the world', commonplace, ordinary.

Qs 16

For each of the examples on the left (A–F), answer the following questions:
1. Identify the IV and DV.
2. Was the task required of participants artificial contrived?
3. Was the study conducted in a natural setting?
4. Was the setting high or low in mundane realism?
5. Did the participants know they were being studied?
6. Were the participants brought into a special (contrived) situation, or did the experimenter go to them?
7. What relevant variables might not have been controlled?
8. Do you think this was a lab or a field experiment?

Field experiments are not all good

Field experiments may be more natural but it is more difficult to control extraneous variables in the 'field'.

There is also a major ethical issue – if participants do not know they are being studied, is it right to manipulate and record their behaviour?

KEY TERMS
Field experiment
Field study
Laboratory experiment
Mundane realism

Validity

Losing sight of the wood for the trees

Does it matter whether an experiment is classified as a field experiment or a lab experiment? No. What matters is an understanding of the bigger picture:

* *Participant awareness.* Awareness factors are threats to **validity**.

* *Experimental control.* Lack of experimental control is a threat to **validity**.

* *Artificiality* (*low mundane realism*) is a threat to **ecological validity** (which we will look at on pages 26 and 27).

The term 'validity' refers to whether something is really measuring what it claims to measure.

The dog hates Maths homework

Every time you start to do your Maths homework your dog starts to howl. You think it's because he doesn't like you doing your maths homework – but this is an invalid effect. Actually it's because the neighbours have a she-dog round every Wednesday evening and as it happens Maths homework is also set on a Wednesday. The same thing happens in psychology experiments!

*The validity of an **experiment** is concerned with whether:*

* The IV produced the change in the DV. Or was the change in the DV caused by something else (an **extraneous** or **confounding variable**)?

* The measurement for the DV is measuring the intended behaviour.

*Validity is **not** whether your results are what you expected.*

*The validity of a **questionnaire** or psychological test is concerned with whether:*

* The questionnaire/test measured what it intended to measure (e.g. health issues) rather than something else (e.g. whether patients like their doctors). See page 45 for more on this.

*The validity of an **observation** is concerned with whether:*

* The system for recording observations allowed the observer to collect all the observations accurately. See page 56 for more on this.

Participant effects

Why don't we want participants to be aware that they are participating in a study? Knowing that you are being studied (increased attention) may act as an alternative IV (a **confounding variable**), as it did in the Hawthorne study. This is known as the **Hawthorne effect** (see page 23).

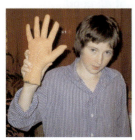

Participants want to offer a helping hand. If they know they are in an experiment, they usually want to please the experimenter and be helpful; otherwise, why are they there? This sometimes results in their being over-cooperative – and behaving artificially.

The opposite effect is also possible when a participant deliberately behaves in such a way as to spoil an experiment. This is sometimes called the '**screw you effect**.'

Social desirability bias is a form of participant reactivity. Participants wish to present themselves in the best possible way and therefore may not behave according to personal preference but behave in the most socially acceptable way for the purposes of a research study.

Demand characteristics create participant effects

We always seek cues about how to behave, particularly in a new environment such as being in an experiment and particularly if a person knows they are in an experiment. Participants actively look for clues as to how they should behave. The result is that they do not behave as they usually would.

Thus, demand characteristics may act as a substitute IV (confounding variable) because they explain the change in the DV.

Participant effects occur because of cues in an experimental situation that may bias a participant's behaviour, e.g. because they know they are being studied or because of demand characteristics.

Demand characteristics are cues in an experimental situation that may unconsciously affect a participant's behaviour.

Dealing with participant effects

Single blind design
The participant does not know the true aims of the experiment or does not know that they are involved in an experiment.

Or the person conducting the experiment (who has not designed it) does not know the aims of the experiment and therefore cannot produce cues about what he or she expects.

Double blind design
Both the participant and the person conducting the experiment (who has not designed it) are 'blind' to the aims.

Experimental realism
If you make the experimental task sufficiently engaging, participants pay attention to the task and not to the fact that they are being observed.

Paying homage to formal terms*

As we have already said, learning about research methods is a bit like learning a foreign language. You have to learn to use a whole new vocabulary, and you have to learn the meaning of this vocabulary. The problem with the vocabulary is that the meaning of the terms is not always black and white. You have to learn to look for the 'general drift' and not be fazed when you find that there are slightly different meanings as your understanding increases.

*An excellent phrase 'invented' by Hugh Coolican (2004a) to explain this problem.

Qs 17

1. *In a study, participants' memory was tested in the morning and in the afternoon to see if there was any difference in their ability to recall numbers.*

   a. Give an example of **one** possible investigator effect in this study.

   b. Describe how you might deal with this investigator effect.

   c. Give an example of how the participant's understanding of the study might affect the findings of this experiment.

   d. Describe how you might deal with this problem of participant reactivity.

   e. Give an example of a possible demand characteristic in this study.

   f. Describe how you might deal with this problem.

2. *A study looked at whether first impressions matter. Participants were given a list of adjectives describing Mr. Smith. One group had positive adjectives first, followed by negative adjectives. The other group had the adjectives in reverse order. They were all then asked to describe Mr Smith.*

   a. Give an example of a possible demand characteristic in this study.

   b. Describe how you might deal with this problem.

Investigator effects

Investigator effects, like participant effects, may reduce the internal validity of an experiment.

Direct effects

An investigator may directly affect a participants' behaviour. This was described in Chapter 1. An investigator might design a study AND conduct it; however, in many experiments the person who designs the experiment is not the same as the minion who actually deals with the participants. To distinguish these roles we talk of investigators and **experimenters**.

It is the person who interacts directly with participants who will be the source of direct investigator effects.

Indirect effects

An investigator may indirectly affect a participant in a number of ways, such as:

- *Investigator experimental design effect:* The investigator may operationalise the measurement of variables in such a way that the desired result is more likely or may limit the duration of the study for the same reason.

- *Investigator loose procedure effect:* The investigator may not clearly specify the standardised instructions and/or procedures which leaves room for the results to be influenced by the experimenter.

Some people take a narrower view and define investigator effects only as the direct effects of an investigator/experimenter on the behaviour of participants rather than the effects of the investigator on the overall design of the experiment.

Investigator effects: *investigator affects participant directly or indirectly (through the design of the study).*

Experimenter effects: *those effects due to direct interaction with the participant.*

Participant reactivity: *participant responds to unconscious cues from the investigator.*

The bottom line ...
Investigator effects are any cues (other than the IV) from an investigator/ experimenter that encourage certain behaviours in the participant, leading to fulfilment of the investigator's expectations. Such cues act as a confounding variable.

KEY TERMS

Demand characteristics
Experimental realism
Participant reactivity
Social desirability bias
Validity

Experimenter bias

This is the term used to describe the effects of an experimenter's expectations on a participant's behaviour. A classic experiment Rosenthal and Fode (1963) showed that even rats are effected by an experimenter's expectations - psychology students were asked train rats to learn their way around a maze. They were told that there were two groups of rats: one group were 'fast learners' having been bred for this characteristic, whilst the other group were 'slow learners'. In fact there were no differences between the rats. Despite this, the findings of the study showed that the supposedly brighter rats actually did better. The only explanaiton can be that the students' expectations affected the rats' performance.

Ecological validity

Can the findings from an experiment be generalised (applied) beyond a particular experiment?

Can we generalise:

- From the experimental setting to different places or settings?

- From the experimental sample to different people or populations?

- From the time of the study (e.g. 1950s) to other times (e.g. the 21st century)?

In other words can we generalise from the experiment to 'real-life'?

Ecological validity (the ability to generalise) will be higher the more you can **replicate** your study and produce the same findings.

Ecological validity is one form of external validity. It is the extent to which the results of an experiment can be generalised from the set of environmental conditions created by the researcher to other environmental conditions – chiefly to 'real life'.

Invariably, studies in psychology involve a trade-off between control and generalisability. Greater control exists in the laboratory. However, it is debatable to what extent findings from the laboratory can be generalised to other environments, especially the less controllable environments in which everyday life is lived.

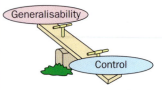

Validity is like a see-saw with control on one side and generalisability on the other.

Explaining ecological validity

Many people mistakenly think that ecological validity means 'the degree to which the behaviours observed and recorded in a study reflect the behaviours that actually occur in natural settings'.

This is not wrong – but it is not right.

1. Part of ecological validity concerns whether a study mirrors the real world. This is **mundane realism**.

2. Part of ecological validity concerns whether participants in a study are **representative** of the target population.

3. Another part of ecological validity concerns '**generalisability**' – the extent to which findings from one study (conducted in a unique setting) can be generalised to other settings (including the 'real world').

Different ecologies

In field research, there is too little control to allow for definite conclusions, whereas in laboratory research, there is too much control to allow for interesting conclusions.

Qs **18**

On this spread and the previous spread a number of key terms and other terms have been highlighted. Use these terms to fill in the blanks below. Each blank may contain one or more words. Some terms may be used more than once, others may not be used at all.

ecological validity, demand characteristics, generalisibility, mundane realism, representativness, validity.

1. *A repeated measures study where participants are able to guess the aim of the study.* This would be a threat to _____.

2. *A study that used an opportunity sample of people living in a city.* This study would lack _____ and _____

3. *A study of 11-year-olds.* This study would lack _____ and _____.

4. *Participants in a lab experiment know they are being studied.* Their performance may improve because of the Hawthorne effect This would affect the _____ of the study.

5. *A study was replicated and the same findings were produced.* This suggests that the study has high _____.

6. Participants want to please an experimenter and therefore respond to _____.

7. Being able to apply the findings of a study to other settings is called _____ .

8. A field experiment is conducted in a more natural setting which may increase its _____ but decrease its _____.

9. _____ is the extent to which behaviours in a study mirror real life.

A study can have mundane realism but lack ecological validity

Consider the following three studies (which you may study during your AS year).

Milgram (1963) Obedience to unjust authority

Forty male participants were told that the study was investigating how punishment affects learning. There were two confederates: an experimenter, and a 'learner'. The participant drew lots with the confederate and always ended up as the 'teacher'. He was told that he must administer increasingly strong electric shocks to the participant each time he got a question wrong. The machine was tested on the participant to show him that it worked.

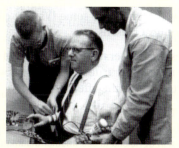

The 'learner' is attached to an electric shock machine by experimenters.

The learner, sitting in another room, gave mainly wrong answers and received his (fake) shocks in silence until they reached 300 volts (a very strong shock). At this point, he pounded on the wall and then gave no response to the next question.

Milgram found that 65% of the participants were fully obedient, i.e. continued to obey up to the maximum voltage of 450 volts.

In later studies, Milgram repeated this set-up using different situations:

* The location was moved to a run-down office (48% obedience).
* The teacher was in the same room as the learner (40% obedience).
* The teacher held the learner's hand on the shock plate (30% obedience).

These replications show that the initial conclusion was correct: situational factors affect obedience to unjust authority.

You might think that the study of nurses by Hofling et al. had high mundane realism and high ecological validity. However, *it had low mundane realism*. Even though it was conducted in a natural setting, the tasks were quite artificial. Rank and Jacobsen's study used *more real-life tasks* – the nurses dealt with a familiar drug and were allowed to consult with each other.

Nevertheless, Hofling et al.'s study was conducted in a more natural setting than Milgram's, although this *does not automatically mean that it had higher ecological validity*. You must always explain why a study has high ecological validity. *The replications of Milgram's study* suggest that his findings do apply to other settings, whereas the same is not true for the study by Hofling et al. Furthermore, *Milgram's study concerned the obedience of ordinary people to perceived authority*, (e.g. obeying an experimenter), so it wasn't really artificial at all.

Furthermore, the doctor–nurse authority relationship is a special one so it is not reasonable to generalise from this to all other kinds of obedience. It is part of a nurse's job to obey orders from doctors, as the nurses in Hofling et al.'s study argued in their defence.

Qs 19

An area of study that has interested psychologists is massed versus distributed practice, i.e. whether learning is better if you practise something repeatedly (massed) or space your periods of practice (distributed). This topic has been studied in different settings.

* *Study 1: Participants were required to recall nonsense syllables on 12 occasions spread over 3 days or 12 days (Jost, 1897). Recall was higher for the 12-day condition. This finding has been supported by subsequent research.*
* *Study 2: Post office workers had to learn to type postcodes either using massed or distributed practice (Baddeley and Longman, 1978). Distributed practice was again found to be superior.*

Present arguments for why each of these studies could be viewed as having high and low ecological validity.

Hofling et al. (1966) Obedience in the real world

Hofling et al. conducted a study in a US hospital. Nurses were telephoned by a 'Dr Smith' who asked that they give 20 mg of a drug called Astroten to a patient. This order contravened hospital regulations in a number of ways:

* Nurses were told not to accept instructions over the phone,
* Nor from an unknown doctor,
* Nor for a dose in excess of the safe amount (the dosage being twice that advised on the bottle),
* Especially for a unknown drug.

Nevertheless, 21 out of 22 (95%) nurses did as requested. When the nurses involved in the study were interviewed afterwards, they said, in their defence, that they had obeyed because that is what doctors expect nurses to do – they behaved as nurses do in real life. Or did they?

Rank and Jacobsen (1977): More nurses

In another study (this time in Australia), nurses were also asked to carry out an irregular order. This time, 16 out of 18 (89%) refused. There were important differences:

* The drug was familiar (Valium).
* The nurses could consult with peers.

The bottom line ...

A study is not high in ecological validity just because it has been carried out in a natural setting. Similarly, it is not low in ecological validity just because it has been conducted in a laboratory.

Ecological validity is established by representativeness and generalisability (some people make the mistake of thinking it is just representativeness).

Ethical issues

In Chapter 1, we considered ethics. There is, however, considerably more to ethics than what was discussed there.

> An **ethical issue** is a conflict between what the researcher wants and the rights of participants. It is a conflict about what is acceptable.

For example, an experimenter might want to study the effects of tattooing on self-esteem. But you cannot tattoo someone without their permission. And even if you did have their permission, there would have to be a very good reason for doing this study in order to justify the procedures used.

I want to find out important things about human behaviour, which means I need to design my experiment in this way.

I have rights.

Ethical issues are like a see-saw.

Deception

Is it acceptable to deceive a participant about the true aims of a study?

From the researcher's point of view, deception is sometimes necessary because otherwise participants might alter their behaviour to fit the experimenter's expectations.

From the participant's point of view, deception is unethical – you should not deceive anyone without good cause. Perhaps more importantly, deception prevents participants being able to give informed consent. They may agree to participate without really knowing what they have let themselves in for, and they might be quite distressed by the experience.

Deception also leads people to see psychologists as untrustworthy. It means that a participant may not want to take part in psychological research in the future.

Informed consent

From the researcher's point of view, informed consent means you have to reveal the true aims of the study – or at least you have to tell participants what is actually going to happen, and then participants are likely to guess the aims.

From the participant's point of view, you should be told what you will be required to do in the study so that you can make an informed decision about whether you wish to participate. This is a basic human right (established during the Nuremburg war trials – Nazi doctors had conducted various experiments on prisoners without their consent).

Protection from physical and psychological harm

From the researcher's point of view, some of the more important questions in psychology involve a degree of distress to participants.

From the participant's point of view, nothing should happen to you during an experiment that will make you less happy, lower your self-esteem or feel embarrassed about your behaviour – i.e. have negative feelings.

Research participants should be protected from undue risk during an investigation. There are many ways in which you can cause harm to participants, some physical (e.g. getting them to smoke, drink alcohol or drink coffee excessively), some psychological (e.g. making them feel inadequate, embarrassing them, etc.).

Normally, the risk of harm must be no greater than in ordinary life.

Participants should be in the same state after an experiment as they were before *unless they have given their informed consent otherwise*.

This is a photograph from Milgram's study of obedience. The participant (playing the role of teacher) is looking serious because he is supposedly delivering a strong electric shock to a 'learner' as he gets an answer wrong.

Do you think that the participant would be unduly distressed by the experience of thinking that he was causing such harm to another? If so, is this 'acceptable' psychological harm?

Confidentiality

From the researcher's point of view, it may be difficult to protect confidentiality because the researcher wishes to publish the findings. A researcher may guarantee *anonymity* (withholding your name), but even then it may be obvious who has been involved in a study. For example, knowing that a study was conducted in St Helena permits some people to be able to identify participants.

From the participant's point of view, the Data Protection Act makes confidentiality a legal right. It is acceptable for personal data to be recorded if the data are not made available in a form that identifies the participants (i.e. confidentiality through anonymity).

Confidentiality and privacy – what's the difference?

The words confidentiality and privacy are sometimes used interchangeably, but there is a distinction between the two.

Confidentiality *concerns the communication of personal information from one person to another, and the trust that this information will then be protected.*

Privacy *refers to a zone of inaccessibility of mind or body, and the trust that this will not be 'invaded'.*

In other words, we have a right of privacy. If this is invaded, confidentiality should be respected.

The right to withdraw

From the researcher's point of view, it may not be possible to offer participants this right, e.g. when conducting a field experiment and participants are not aware they are being studied.

From the participant's point of view, if you have been deceived about the aims of the study you still ought to have the option to quit if you find that you do not like what is going on. This compensates for the fact that you did not give informed consent. Even with informed consent, you may not fully understand what is involved.

Privacy

From the researcher's point of view, it may be difficult to avoid invasion of privacy in a field experiment.

From the participant's point of view, people do not expect to be observed by others in certain situations. We have a right to privacy.

In one study, psychologists investigated invasion of personal space by conducting a field experiment in a urinal. There were three conditions: a confederate stood either immediately next to a participant or one urinal away, or was absent. The experimenter recorded micturation times (how long they took to pee) as an indication of how comfortable the participant felt (Middlemist *et al.*, 1976).
Is it unacceptable to observe people in such a place?

Qs   22

1. Do you think that participants in Milgram's study would have been unduly distressed by taking part?
2. If they were distressed, do you think that this is acceptable?
3. Do you think it is unacceptable to observe people in a public urinal?
4. In Milgram's experiment, do think it was acceptable to deceive his participants?
5. Did Milgram obtain informed consent from his participants? Explain your answer.
6. Did Milgram give participants the right to withdraw from his experiment? Explain your answer.

More on Milgram

The participants in Milgram's study were told that it concerned the effect of punishment on learning. They were asked for their consent to take part and told they would be paid $4.50 for taking part. Furthermore, they were told that they could withdraw from the experiment at any time and would still be paid for having taken part.

During the experiment, if a participant asked to stop, the experimenter had been instructed to deliver a set of 'prods' such as saying, 'It is absolutely essential that you continue' or 'You have no other choice; you must go on'.

Does this count as informed consent?

Does this count as the right to withdraw?

KEY TERMS

Confidentiality
Deception
Ethics
Informed consent
Privacy
Protection from harm
Right to withdraw

Experimental and control groups

A researcher might want to investigate the effect that rewards have on performance. To do this, children are asked to collect rubbish from a playground and offered a chocolate bar as a reward. They collect several bags of rubbish.

We cannot conclude anything about the effects of the reward because all the children were told that they would receive a reward. We need to have a control group so that we can make a comparison.

We need two groups: an **experimental group** (offered a reward) and a **control group** (offered no reward). This allows us to compare the effects of the reward (IV) on collecting rubbish (the DV).

Or we need to have two conditions: an **experimental condition** (children offered a reward on one occasion) and a **control condition** (offered no reward on another occasion).

Threats to validity

If there is an experimental group and a control group, it is possible that the experimental group will perform differently for reasons other than the IV (experimental treatment).

Consider a study on the effectiveness of a new teaching programme. One class is taught using the new programme (experimental group) and compared with another class taught using the 'old' programme (control group).

- The experimental group might improve simply because the teaching programme is new.
- The classes may have had different teachers.
- Or the control group might try extra hard to show that the old way is just as good or better than the new approach. This is called the **John Henry effect**.

John Henry is an American legend. He worked on building the railroads, drilling holes by hitting thick steel spikes into rocks. There was no one who could match him, although many tried.

Then one day someone tried to sell a steam-powered drill to the railroad company, claiming that it could out-drill any man. They set up a contest between John Henry and that drill. The foreman ran the newfangled steam drill. John Henry pulled out two 20 pound hammers, one in each hand. They drilled and drilled, dust rising everywhere. The men were howling and cheering. At the end of 35 minutes, John Henry had drilled two 7-foot holes – a total of 14 feet, whereas the steam drill had only drilled one 9-foot hole.

Thinking back to Milgram and Hofling

After Milgram's research, another study found real-life support for the findings. Dicks (1972) interviewed former German soldiers and found that they displayed the same psychological mechanisms of obedience shown by participants in laboratory-based obedience research. However, one event of the Second World War found the opposite (Mandel, 1998). In an encounter between German troops and civilians, the commander, Major Trapp, had orders to kill all the Jews in a small town – but Trapp told his men that, if they did not wish to obey orders, he would assign them to other duties. Nevertheless, most of the men did obey – despite the fact that, according to Milgram, the task involved many of the factors that should lead to reduced obedience (face-to-face contact, some disobedient peers, absence of pressure from an authority figure).

This challenges our original conclusion because now it appears that Milgram's findings have not been replicated in other settings.

The moral of the story: Don't assume that any study has **ecological validity** – search for confirming evidence. All research conducted in the real world is not automatically ecologically valid, and all laboratory studies are not automatically ecologically *invalid*. Every study has some ecological validity – some are just more ecologically valid than others.

> **KEY TERMS**
> Control group/condition
> Experimental group/condition

Qs 24

A playgroup wishes to investigate whether children play differently if an adult is present or not.

1. Describe how you might design a study to investigate this using an independent groups design.
2. Which is the experimental group and which is the control group?
3. Identify **one or more** ethical issues and suggest how you would deal with these.
4. To what extent would the findings of your study have representativeness?
5. To what extent would the findings of your study have generalisability?
6. How could you conduct a study with the same aims using a repeated measures design?
7. Identify the experimental and control conditions in this new study.
8. Describe **one** advantage and **one** disadvantage of using a repeated measures design in this study.

Activity 8 — What is validity all about?

Using what you have learned in this chapter, create something to represent the various aspects of validity. It could be a PowerPoint presentation, a mobile, a poster for your classroom, a leaflet, a cartoon strip, a poem, a rap song – anything that is entertaining AND forces you to process the material (as processing leads to deeper understanding and long-term memories).

YOU ARE NOW READY TO DO ACTIVITY C, **SEE PAGE** 80.

Multiple choice questions

1. **Which of the following is *not* a characteristic of a field experiment?**
   a. It is conducted in a natural environment.
   b. The IV is directly manipulated by the experimenter.
   c. Extraneous variables can be well controlled.
   d. Participants are often not aware that they are being studied.

2. **Which of the following is *not* a characteristic of a lab experiment?**
   a. It is conducted in a natural environment.
   b. The IV is directly manipulated by the experimenter.
   c. Extraneous variables can be well controlled.
   d. Participants are often aware that they are being studied.

3. **Mundane realism refers to**
   a. Using video film to capture participants' behaviour.
   b. An experiment being boring and therefore not holding the participant's interest.
   c. The extent to which an experiment mirrors the real world.
   d. A Spanish football team.

4. **Variables in an experiment are operationalised, which means they are**
   a. Understandable to participants.
   b. Used in a medical experiment.
   c. Described in a way that can be easily measured or manipulated.
   d. Turned into numbers.

5. **Lab experiments are sometimes artificial because**
   a. Participants know they are being studied and this may affect their behaviour.
   b. The setting may lack mundane realism.
   c. The IV may be operationalised in such a way that it does not represent real-life experiences.
   d. All of the above.

6. **Validity is concerned with**
   a. Having an IV and DV
   b. The consistency of measurement.
   c. Whether a study is measuring what it claims to measure.
   d. Whether the findings are what the experimenter expected.

7. **Ecological validity refers to**
   a. The generalisability of research findings to real-life situations.
   b. Whether the findings are what the experimenter expected.
   c. Whether an observed effect can be attributed to the IV.
   d. All of the above.

8. **Which of the following is *not* a kind of external validity?**
   a. Ecological validity.
   b. Mundane validity.
   c. Population validity.
   d. Historical validity.

9. **Demand characteristics are**
   a. Features of an experiment that cannot be controlled.
   b. Threats to external validity.
   c. Problem behaviours.
   d. Cues in an experimental situation that unconsciously affect a participant's behaviour.

10. **Which of the following would *not* be a threat to internal validity?**
    a. Experimenter bias.
    b. Participant reactivity.
    c. Social desirability bias.
    d. Single-blind design.

11. **The person who designs an experiment is called the**
    a. Investigator.
    b. Experimenter.
    c. Participant.
    d. Designer.

12. **An investigator effect is any effect the investigator has on**
    a. An investigation.
    b. Participants' behaviour.
    c. Extraneous variables.
    d. All of the above.

13. **Ecological validity concerns**
    a. Representativeness.
    b. Generalisability.
    c. Representativeness and reliability.
    d. Representativeness and generalisability.

14. **Which of the following is the best definition of ecological validity?**
    a. Ecological validity is the degree to which behaviour in the laboratory reflects real life.
    b. Ecological validity is the extent to which findings can be generalised from the lab to the real world.
    c. Ecological validity is the extent to which findings can be generalised from the experimental setting to other settings.
    d. Ecological validity is the degree to which findings can be generalised from one group of people to the target population.

15. **If the participants in a study are only men, we might think the study had low**
    a. Population validity.
    b. Ecological validity.
    c. External validity.
    d. Both a and c.

16. **In a natural experiment**
    a. The IV is controlled by an experimenter.
    b. The IV varies naturally.
    c. The DV is controlled by an experimenter.
    d. The DV varies naturally.

17. **Natural experiments are not 'true' experiments because**
    a. Participants are not randomly allocated to conditions.
    b. The sample studied may have unique characteristics.
    c. The IV is not directly manipulated by the experimenter.
    d. All of the above.

18. **Studies that compare the behaviour of males and females (gender studies) are**
    a. Difference studies.
    b. Field experiments.
    c. Natural experiments.
    d. Both a and c.

19. **Debriefing is**
    a. An ethical issue.
    b. An ethical guideline.
    c. An ethical issue and an ethical guideline.
    d. A folder for research notes.

20. **If informed consent is not possible, a possible alternative is to**
    a. Give participants the right to withdraw.
    b. Debrief participants.
    c. Obtain presumptive consent.
    d. All of the above.

Contents

Self-report measures

questionnaires, interviews and studies using correlational analysis

DIY: A study using a correlational analysis

ESP: A 'sheep–goat effect'

People who believe in paranormal phenomena are the 'sheep'.

People who do not believe in paranormal phenomena are the 'goats'.

Various studies have looked at the relationship between paranormal beliefs and misjudgements of probability, e.g. that of Brugger *et al.* (1990). People who are sheep (believe in paranormal phenomena) are less good at probabilistic reasoning. Probabilistic reasoning refers to making judgements related to probability. For example, which is more likely:

- I throw 10 dice at the same time and get 10 sixes?
- I throw one dice 10 times in succession and get 10 successive sixes?

In fact, they are both equally likely – if you did not think so, it suggests you are not good at probabilistic reasoning. You probably also think you should never choose the numbers in the lottery that came up last time.

The link between probabilistic reasoning and paranormal belief is that some people like to have an explanation for the things that happen around them. For example, if a door bangs shut on a windless night, such people 'prefer' the explanation that there was a ghost, whereas others prefer to accept that there is no explanation. Those preferring the explanation of causes also do not find it easy to comprehend the idea of chance (probability).

A final word on correlation

The correlations we have looked at are all **linear** – in a perfect positive correlation (+1) all the values would lie in a *straight* line from the bottom left to the top right.

There is, however, a different kind of correlation – **a curvilinear correlation**. The relationship is not linear – it is curved – but there is still a predictable relationship. For example, stress and performance do not have a linear relationship. Performance on many tasks is depressed when stress is too high or too low; it is best when stress is moderate. The relationship between stress and performance was first identified by Yerkes and Dodson and thus called the Yerkes–Dodson Law. The graph on the right illustrates this relationship.

 Activity 13 — Investigating the sheep–goat effect

To investigate this, you need:

1. A measure of the degree to which someone believes in paranormal phenomena.

   You can use The Belief in the Paranormal Scale (on page 48) or produce your own questionnaire. A high score on the scale indicates that you believe in paranormal phenomena.

2. A measure of probabilistic reasoning.

   Ask participants to mimic the rolling of a dice by writing or saying a digit between 1 and 6. They should produce a string of 100 numbers.

   The way to score this is printed at the bottom of page 48. A high score indicates that they are not good at probabilistic reasoning.

 To analyse your data

1. Draw a scattergraph to show the relationship between the co-variables (belief in the paranormal and probabilistic reasoning).

2. Calculate the correlation coefficient.

   What do the graph and correlation coefficient tell you about your findings? Is the correlation strong, moderate or weak?

3. Calculate the mean, median and mode for both sets of data (belief in the paranormal and probabilistic reasoning).

   Which measure of central tendency is the most useful? Why?

   Which measure of central tendency is the least useful? Why?

4. Sort your participants into three groups: sheep, goats and neutral. You need to decide how to define each group; e.g. you might decide that the sheep are all those who scored more than 45.

   Draw a bar chart to show the mean probabilistic reasoning score for each group.

   Compare the scattergraph and the bar chart. Which do you think is more informative?

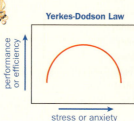

Yerkes-Dodson Law

performance or efficiency

stress or anxiety

Qs 31

1. Describe the aims of the sheep–goat study.
2. Would the hypothesis predict a positive or a negative correlation?
3. What conclusions can you draw from your findings?

> **YOU ARE NOW READY TO DO**
> ACTIVITY D, **SEE PAGE** 88.

ACTIVITY D, **SEE PAGE** 88.

KEY TERMS

Curvilinear correlation
Linear correlation

Multiple choice questions

1. Data related to how people think and feel are called
   a. Qualitative data.
   b. Quantitative data.
   c. Questionnaire data.
   d. Both a and c.

2. Data that can be easily counted are called
   a. Qualitative data.
   b. Quantitative data.
   c. Questionnaire data.
   d. Both a and c.

3. Closed questions tend to produce
   a. Qualitative data.
   b. Quantitative data.
   c. Questionnaire data.
   d. Both a and c.

4. Open questions tend to produce
   a. Qualitative data.
   b. Quantitative data.
   c. Questionnaire data.
   d. Both a and c.

5. Respondents often answer questions in a way that makes them look good rather than being truthful. This is called
   a. A response set.
   b. A leading question.
   c. Social desirability bias.
   d. The Hawthorne effect.

6. One means of assessing people's attitudes is by using a scale from strongly agree to strongly disagree. This is called
   a. The semantic differential technique.
   b. A forced choice scale.
   c. A quantitative scale.
   d. The Likert Scale.

7. Which of the following is *not* an advantage of qualitative data?
   a. Represent thoughts and feelings that cannot be measured in an experiment.
   b. Easy to analyse the findings.
   c. Represents the true complexity of human behaviour.
   d. Means that unexpected information can be collected.

8. A clinical interview is a kind of
   a. Questionnaire.
   b. Structured interview.
   c. Unstructured interview.
   d. Correlation.

9. One advantage of an interview in comparison with a questionnaire is
   a. The interviewer can adapt questions as he or she goes along.
   b. People may feel more comfortable about revealing personal information.
   c. Interviews can be delivered by less skilled personnel.
   d. Social desirability bias is less of a problem.

10. Which of the following is false?
    a. A questionnaire can collect data from a large number of people in a short space of time.
    b. Questionnaires are less easy to analyse than interviews.
    c. Questionnaires do not require specialist administrators.
    d. Social desirability bias is a problem in a questionnaire.

11. A leading question is a question that
    a. Contains the answer in the question.
    b. Is the most important question on a questionnaire.
    c. Suggests what answer is desired.
    d. Tends to confuse respondents.

12. In a correlation you have
    a. An IV and a DV.
    b. Co-variables.
    c. Factors.
    d. Both a and b.

13. A negative correlation is when
    a. Two variables increase together.
    b. As one variable increases, the other decreases.
    c. There is a weak correlation between two variables.
    d. There is a strong correlation between two variables.

14. A correlation coefficient of +0.65 indicates.
    a. No correlation.
    b. A weak positive correlation.
    c. A moderate positive correlation.
    d. A strong positive correlation.

15. Which of the following could *not* be a correlation coefficient?
    a. 0
    b. +0.79
    c. +1.28
    d. −0.30

16. A scattergraph is
    a. A descriptive statistic.
    b. A graph that illustrates a correlation.
    c. A collection of dots where each dot represents a pair of scores.
    d. All of the above.

17. Which of the following is *not* an advantage of a study using a correlational analysis?
    a. Can be used when it is unethical or impractical to manipulate variables.
    b. Useful to help decide whether a more rigorous scientific investigation into the apparent relationship is justified.
    c. If no correlation can be found, you can rule out a causal relationship.
    d. Can demonstrate a causal relationship.

18. Internal reliability is a measure of the extent to which
    a. One measure of an object varies from another measure of the same object.
    b. How true or legitimate a measurement is.
    c. You obtain the result you were expecting.
    d. Something is consistent within itself.

19. One way to assess internal reliability is to
    a. Replicate the study.
    b. Use the test-retest method.
    c. Use the split-half method.
    d. Ask a friend.

20. Face validity is an assessment of whether a test
    a. Looks appealing to participants.
    b. Looks like it is measuring what it intends to measure.
    c. Produces a score similar to the score produced by another test measuring the same thing.
    d. All of the above.

OBSERVATIONS AND A FEW OTHER THINGS

Contents

Observations
and a few other things

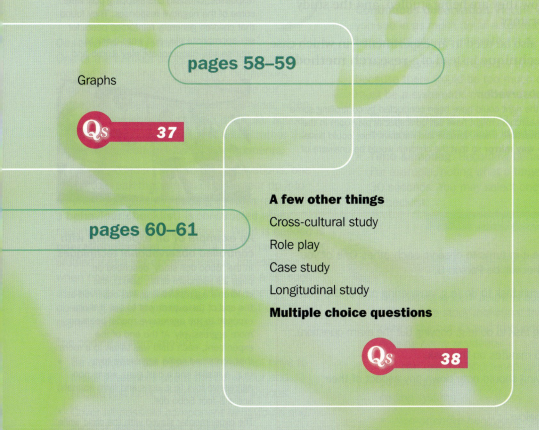

Observational studies

Distinctions

Method and technique

Remember that all research involves making observations; however, in the case of some research, the overall *method* is observational, where the emphasis is on observing a relatively unconstrained segment of a person's freely chosen behaviour.

Controlled and naturalistic

In both cases, systematic methods are used to record observations. In a controlled observation, the environmental variables are controlled to some extent e.g. the setting may be moved from the person's normal environment, or some of the items in the environment may be deliberately chosen.

Participant and non-participant

In many cases, the observer is merely watching the behaviour of others and acts as a non-participant. In some studies, observers also participate, which may affect their objectivity. A classic example of a participant observation is described on the right.

Disclosed and undisclosed (overt and covert)

One-way mirrors are used to prevent participants being aware that they are being observed. This is called undisclosed (covert) observation. Knowing that your behaviour is being observed is likely to alter your behaviour. Observers often try to be as unobtrusive as possible.

Direct and indirect

In many studies, observations are made of data that have already been collected, e.g. observing advertisements on TV to see what gender bias exists, or observing newspaper advertisements or children's books. This is indirect observation (see 'Content analysis' on page 57).

Core Study David Rosenhan had a hunch that, in the 1970s, psychiatrists were not very good at consistently telling the difference between people who are sane and people who are insane. He decided that participant observation would be the ideal way to investigate this. Thus, eight people (friends of Rosenhan) posed as pseudo-patients. Each made an appointment at a mental hospital, told the psychiatrist of a voice in their head saying 'empty', 'hollow' and 'thud'. All were admitted to mental hospital, proceeded to act entirely normally but were detained in hospital for on average 19 days (one remaining for 52 days) until finally discharged. During their stay they interacted with their fellow patients, followed the ward's activities and asked staff about when they might be discharged. The pseudo-patients witnessed the treatment of patients by staff (sometimes very inhumane and violent and frequently uncaring), as well as experiencing at first hand the overwhelming sense of powerlessness. Being a participant observer allowed the pseudo-patients to identify with their fellow patients' experience and collect a rich source of data (Rosenhan, 1973).

"One flew over the Cuckoo's Nest" – famous depiction of mental hospitals in the 1970's

Devices for managing and recording observations

The raw data gathered in an observational study can come in visual, audio or written form. To assist the collection of data you might use:

- Binoculars, if you are observing from any distance.
- One-way mirrors, for undisclosed observations.
- A video camera, if you want to replay behavioural sequences or observe people in an unobtrusive manner.
- An audio-cassette recorder, again for replaying sequences so they can be coded later.
- Paper for recording data using a coding system, this can be done 'live' or using video/audio-recording.

Analysing observational data

Unstructured observations produce **qualitative** data.

Structured or systematic observations produce numerical data in categories (**quantitative**) that can be analysed using descriptive statistics.

Qs

33

1. Identify what kind of observational study was conducted by Rosenhan. (described top right).

2. In each of the following observations, state which sampling procedure would be most appropriate and explain how you would do it:

   a. Recording instances of aggressive behaviour in children playing in a school playground.

   b. Vocalisations (words, sounds) made by young children.

   c. Compliance with controlled pedestrian crossings by pedestrians.

   d. Litter-dropping in a public park.

   e. Behaviour of dog owners when walking their dogs.

3. *A group of students decided to study student behaviour in the school library.*

   a. Suggest **one or more** hypotheses that you might investigate.

   b. List **five** behaviours you might include in a behaviour checklist.

   c. Identify a suitable sampling procedure and explain how you would do it.

   d. How could you observe the students so that they were not aware that they were being observed?

   e. What ethical issues might be raised in this observational study?

   f. For each issue identified in your answer to (e), explain how you could deal with this issue and whether this would be acceptable.

   g. Explain in what way this would be a naturalistic observation.

   h. In this study, is observation a method or a technique?

4. *What distinguishes a successful teacher from an unsuccessful one? A group of students decide to observe various teachers while they are teaching.*

   a. Identify **two** ways in which you could operationalise 'successful teaching behaviour'.

   b. Describe **one** way in which you could minimise the intrusive nature of your observations.

   c. How would you record the data in this observational study?

   d. Suggest **one** advantage and **one** disadvantage of conducting an observational study in this context.

   e. Describe **two** ways of ensuring that this study would be carried out in an ethically acceptable manner.

   f. In this study, is observation a method or a technique?

Reliability

Observations should be consistent, which means that two observers should ideally produce the same record. The extent to which two (or more) observers agree is called inter-rater or **inter-observer reliability**. This is measured by correlating the observations of two or more observers (see 'Assessing reliability' below). A general rule is that if (Total agreements) ÷ (Total observations) > 0.80, the data have inter-observer reliability.

Dealing with low reliability

Observers should be trained in the use of a coding system/behaviour checklist. They should practise using it and discuss their observations.

Validity

Observational studies are likely to have high **ecological validity** because they involve more natural behaviours (but remember the discussion in Chapter 2 – naturalness does not always mean greater ecological validity).

Validity may be low, for example, children are observed only in middle-class homes. The findings may not generalise to all children.

Observations will not be valid (or reliable) if the coding system/behaviour checklist is flawed. For example, some observations may belong in more than one category, or some behaviours may not be codeable.

The validity of observations is also affected by **observer bias** – what someone observes is influenced by their expectations. This reduces the objectivity of observations.

Dealing with low validity

Conducting observations in varied settings with varied participants.

Dealing with low reliability

Using more than one observer to reduce observer bias and averaging data across observers (balances out any biases).

Ethical issues

In a naturalistic observation, participants may be observed without their **informed consent**.

Some observations may be regarded as an invasion of **privacy**. Participant **confidentiality** should be respected.

The use of one-way mirrors involves **deception**/lack of informed consent.

Dealing with ethical issues

Informed consent: In some cases, it may be possible to obtain informed consent. For example, in the observations of nursery children by the BEO (see below left), parental permission was obtained for all children attending the nursery.

Invasion of privacy: **Ethical guidelines** generally advise that it is acceptable to observe people in public places (places where people expect to be seen by others).

Ethical committees can be used to approve observational designs.

Qs 34

1. On the left are two graphs showing the observations of two children by three observers. Do you think that the graphs indicate an acceptable level of inter-observer reliability?

2. *A psychologist decided to observe the non-verbal behaviours between two people having a conversation. (Non-verbal behaviours are those which do not involve language – such as smiling, touching, etc.)*

   a. Explain why it would be desirable to conduct a pilot study.

   b. If this is to be a naturalistic observation, *where* should the student researchers make their observations?

   c. Each conversation is observed by two students. Identify **one** way in which you could ensure reliability between the different observers and explain how you might put this into practice.

   d. Describe **two** features of the study that might threaten its validity.

   e. Explain how you could deal with these two features that might threaten validity.

   f. Draw a suitable table for recording observations, showing some of the possible categories.

   g. Describe **one** way of ensuring that this study would be carried out in an ethically acceptable manner.

   h. Evaluate your method of dealing with ethics.

Training observers

The Behavioural Observation unit (BEO) at the University of Bern trains people in the use of observational techniques (BEO, 2004). They have a nursery school at the unit where the children can be observed through a one-way mirror. The data collected have been used for various studies such as comparing twins. The unit has devised a coding system (called KaSo 12):

No social participation
1. Occupied alone
2. Hanging around alone
3. Alone – onlooker
4. Alone – unclear
Social participation
5. Parallel behaviour 1
6. Parallel behaviour 2
7. Loosely associated but interactive
8. Role play – identifiable
9. Social participation unclear
Not identifiable
10. Child not in view, generally unclear

Assessing reliability

The graph below show observations made of two children in the nursery class using KaSo 12. Each time, three observers were used (blue, red and green lines). The figures represent the relative duration of a specific behaviour category in per cent.

Child 1: Mean correlation of the 3 profiles: *r* = 0.86.

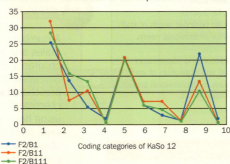

F2/B1
F2/B11
F2/B111
Coding categories of KaSo 12

Child 2: Showing a markedly different distribution of behaviour patterns but an even closer correlation: *r* = 0.93.

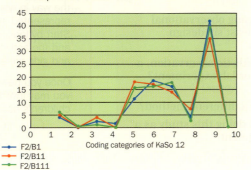

F2/B1
F2/B11
F2/B111
Coding categories of KaSo 12

KEY TERMS
Inter-observer reliability
Non-participant observation
Observer bias

OBSERVATIONS AND A FEW OTHER THINGS

Task 1

On the right are a variety of graphs. For each one, identify the type of graph and describe one or more conclusions that could be drawn from the graph.

Task 2

A psychology class conduct a study on memory. Each student does a memory test first thing in the morning and then again in the afternoon. The table below shows how many items they got correct each time.

Student	1	2	3	4	5	6	7	8	9	10
Morning test	18	20	17	16	19	22	21	19	15	13
Afternoon test	20	18	15	12	18	20	16	16	17	14

(a) Calculate the mean, median, mode and range for each data set.

(b) What measure of central tendency would be most suitable to use to describe this data? Explain your answer.

(c) What measure of dispersion would be most suitable to use to describe this data? Explain your answer.

(d) Draw both a histogram and a scattergraph to represent the data from this study.

(e) From studying your graphs, what conclusions could you draw about this data?

Task 3

In this book, we have covered seven methods of research. Now let's see what you can remember!

When writing about strengths and weaknesses, try as far as possible to state a strength/weakness that is particular to the method, not one that could be applied to any method.

Research method	Two strengths	Two weaknesses	Two possible ethical issues
Lab experiment			
Field experiment			
Natural experiment			
Questionnaire			
Interview			
Investigation using a correlational analysis			
Naturalistic observation			

Task 4

You may recall that, right at the beginning of the book, there was a note on how learning about research methods was a bit like learning a foreign language – you have to learn a new set of words and what they mean. The best way to do this is to *use* your new language. The exercises throughout this book were intended to help you do this.

Write down now all the new words you have learned (those you can remember) and then check through your Research Methods Booklet to see what words you have forgotten. You might also check to see which terms were commonly forgotten. In fact, there's lots of scope for further analysis!

You might work with a partner and, when you have finished, get another pair to check your list. See who in the class can correctly identify the most terms. You could even record the results in a bar chart!

Task 5

Test a friend on the key terms (or other terms). Read out a definition and see whether your friend can give the right term, You can do this using your OCR student workbook or the glossary at the end of this book. Or you can even make a game by constructing cards with the definitions on one side and the term on the reverse. (See 'Supplementary materials' on the Nelson Thornes website (www.nelsonthornes.com/researchmethods) for a Word file of the glossary.)

Task 6

Now that you have (just about) finished research methods, you could look back to the topic you found most challenging. To help you understand this better, create something memorable (for you and your class mates). It could be a PowerPoint® presentation, a mobile, a poster for your classroom, a cartoon strip, a poem or even a rap.

1

Graph showing IQ score and age

(bar chart: IQ on y-axis from 105 to 114; Age in years on x-axis with categories 16–25, 26–40, 41–59, 60+. Bars at approximately 108, 112, 113, 112.)

2

(a)

Content analysis of lonely hearts ads:
People seeking resources
(from Waynforth and Dunbar, 1995)

(bar chart: Number of advertisers (%) on y-axis 0 to 30; Age in years on x-axis with categories 20–29, 30–39, 40–49, 50–59, 60–69. Women and Men bars.)

■ Women ■ Men

3

Graph showing pet ownership and sex of owner

(bar chart: Number of people on y-axis 0 to 8; x-axis categories 0, 1, 2, 3, 4, 5. Men and Women bars.)

■ Men
■ Women

(b)

Lonely hearts offering attractiveness

(bar chart: Number of advertisers (%) on y-axis 0 to 30; Age in years on x-axis with categories 20–29, 30–39, 40–49, 50–59, 60–69.)

4

Driving under the influence of an illicit drug,
reported by people of different ages

(scatter plot: Percentage on y-axis 0 to 80; Age in years on x-axis 0 to 80.)

5

Racial violence and economic conditions
in the years 1882–1915

(bar chart: Number of incidents of racial violence per year on y-axis 0 to 120; Value of cotton in millions of dollars on x-axis with categories 250–450, 450–650, 650–800.)

6

IQ and the importance of religion to individuals' lives

(scatter plot: IQ on y-axis 60 to 110; Religion important (%) on x-axis 0 to 100.)

7

The relationship between final test mark
and time spent on the test

(scatter plot: English score (%) on y-axis 0 to 90; Time taken (minutes) on x-axis 0 to 40.)

8

Reduction in anxiety:
combined data from 99 studies

(bar chart: Anxiety levels measured by units of cortisol in urine on y-axis from -.6 to .2; categories Combined psychological and drug therapy, Psychological therapy, Drug therapy, Placebo.)

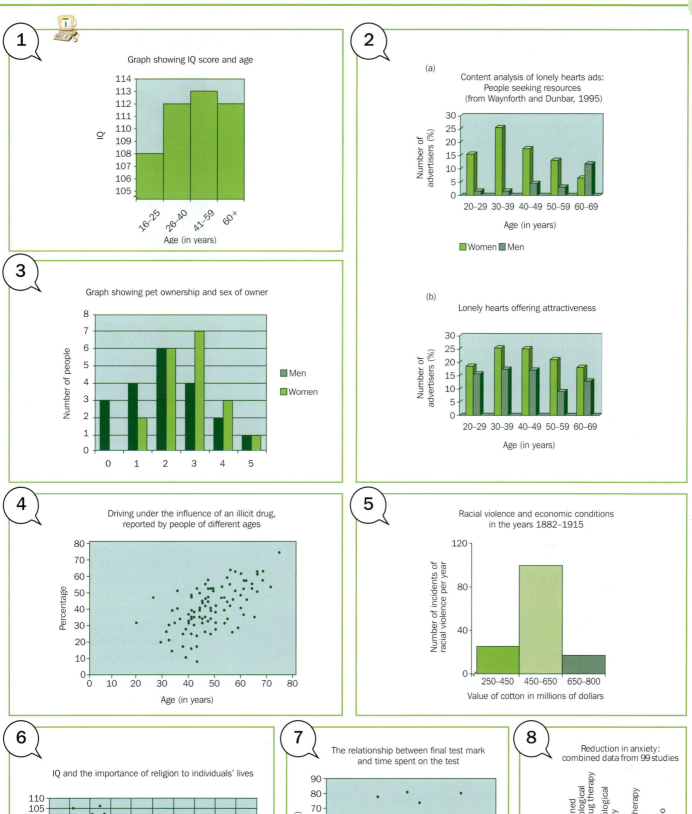

A few other things

This book only covers some of the research methods and some of the designs that are used by psychologists. On this page, we will very briefly mention some other methods and designs. These are the ones you are likely to encounter when you read about research in psychology, and it is useful to know something about them and their plus and minus points.

Cross-cultural study

Psychologists quite often compare behaviours in different cultures and make comparisons across cultures, for example the OCR core study by Deregowski (1972). This is a way of seeing whether cultural practices affect behaviour. It is a kind of **natural experiment** in which the IV is, for example, child-rearing techniques in different cultures and the DV is some behaviour, such as attachment. This enables researchers to see if the DV is due to child-rearing techniques.

☹ There are many limitations to such studies. For example, researchers may use tests or procedures that have been developed in the US and are not valid in the other culture. This may make the individuals in the other culture appear 'abnormal' or inferior. The term that is used to describe this is an *imposed ethic* – when a technique or psychological test is used in one culture even though it was designed for use in another culture.

☹ A second limitation is that the group of participants may not be representative of that culture, yet we make generalisations about the whole culture – or even the whole country.

Qs **38**

In each of the following, identify the research method and, where relevant, the research technique(s) or design.

1. Scores from a questionnaire 'How good is your memory' are related to GCSE results.
2. A male or female confederate stands by the roadside with broken-down car to see if people are more likely to help a male or female.
3. Psychology A level results from two classes are compared to see if Teacher A's teaching style was better than that of Teacher B.
4. Children are shown two films: one that shows a child being helpful and another that shows a child not being helpful. They then are given free play time to see if they are more helpful.
5. Students are asked to explain what methods they find most successful for revision.
6. Interactions between first-time mothers and their newborn babies are compared with the interactions of mothers having a second baby.
7. A study on gambling is based around the experiences of one individual.

Longitudinal study

When a study is conducted over a long period of time it is said to have a **longitudinal study** (it's long!). The need for such studies is to be able to observe long-term effects and to make comparisons between the same individual at different ages. The OCR core study by Hodges and Tizard (1989) is an example of a study with a longitudinal design as the children were studied at various times up until the age of 16.

An alternative way to study behaviour is called a **snapshot study** (which takes a lot less time). In this case one group of participants of a young age are compared with another, older group of participants, for example in Samuel and Bryant's (1984) study of conservation.

☺ The advantage of using a longitudinal study is that **participant** variables are controlled. In a snapshot study the advantage is that the two groups of participants may be quite different and then differences between groups may be due to participant variables rather than the independent variable.

☹ **Attrition** is a problem when using a longitudinal design. This refers to the likelihood that some participants drop-out over time and it is likely that it is particular kinds of participants who drop out and this results in a biased sample.

In Zimbardo's classic study of obedience and conformity, participants were required to play the roles of prisoners or guards (Zimbardo *et al.*, 1973).

Role Play

In some investigations, participants are told to take on a certain role and their behaviour can then be observed as if it were real life. For example, they might be asked to imagine that they are lying, or to pretend that they are a prison guard. This is a form of **controlled observational study**.

☺ This enables researchers to control certain variables so real-life behaviour can be studied that might otherwise be impractical or unethical to observe.

☹ The question is whether people really do act as they would in real life. In Zimbardo's study, the participants acting as guards might have been following what they *thought* was guard-like behaviour, as seen in films. If they had been real-life guards, they might have acted more in accordance with personal principles rather than according to social norms.

Case study

A case study is a research investigation that involves the detailed study of a single individual, institution or event, for example the OCR core studies by Gardner and Gardner (1969) and Thigpen and Cleckley (1954).

☺ Case studies concern unique individuals or cases. The opportunity to study one case permits us to record rich details of human experience.

☹ It is, however, difficult to generalise from such individual cases and hard to uncover what did actually happen in the past.

KEY TERMS

Case study
Cross-cultural study
Longitudinal study
Role play
Snapshot study

Multiple choice questions

1. **Observation is a**
   a. Research method.
   b. Research technique.
   c. Form of experiment.
   d. Both a and b.

2. **The key feature of a naturalistic observation is that**
   a. No set categories are used to record behaviour.
   b. Behaviour is observed.
   c. There is an IV.
   d. Everything has been left as it normally is.

3. **A coding system is a method used in observational research for**
   a. Sampling behaviours.
   b. Making systematic observations.
   c. Analysing the findings.
   d. All of the above.

4. **Which of the following is *not* a method of sampling observations?**
   a. Continuous observation.
   b. Event sampling.
   c. Microscopic sampling.
   d. Time sampling.

5. **Event sampling involves**
   a. Noting what a target individual is doing every 30 seconds.
   b. Keeping a count of each time a target behaviour occurs.
   c. Making notes on all behaviours that occur.
   d. Noting what everyone is doing at a point in time.

6. **A disclosed observation is where**
   a. Observers do not participate in the study.
   b. Observers are also participants in the study.
   c. Participants know they are being observed.
   d. Participants do not know they are being observed.

7. **When observations are made from data in a newspaper, this is called**
   a. Direct observation.
   b. Indirect observation.
   c. Content analysis.
   d. Both b and c.

8. **The reliability of observations may be affected by:**
   a. Lack of agreement between several observers when observing the same thing.
   b. Lack of agreement between observations made by one observer on several occasions.
   c. Lack of agreement between several observers when observing different things.
   d. Both a and b.

9. **The validity of observations may be affected by**
   a. Observer bias.
   b. Low inter-observer reliability.
   c. Limited sample of participants.
   d. All of the above.

10. **Low reliability can be dealt with by**
    a. Using more than one observer.
    b. Conducting observations in varied settings with varied participants.
    c. Training observers to use the coding system.
    d. Both a and b.

11. **Low validity can be dealt with by**
    a. Using more than one observer.
    b. Conducting observations in varied settings with varied participants.
    c. Training observers to use the coding system.
    d. Both a and b.

12. **Inter-observer reliability is the extent to which**
    a. Two or more observers produce the same observations.
    b. Observers are not biased in the judgements they make.
    c. Observers do not drop out during an observational study.
    d. Both a and b.

13. **Which of the following ethical issues is *not* likely to be a problem in a naturalistic observation?**
    a. Informed consent.
    b. Privacy.
    c. Confidentiality.
    d. Protection from psychological harm.

14. **Which of the following is *not* a weakness of a naturalistic observation?**
    a. Provides a less realistic picture of behaviour.
    b. Data are difficult to collect.
    c. Cannot investigate cause and effect.
    d. The method requires careful training.

15. **Role play is a kind of**
    a. Naturalistic observation.
    b. Controlled observation.
    c. Field experiment.
    d. Natural experiment.

16. **A case study may concern**
    a. A single individual.
    b. An institution.
    c. An event.
    d. All of the above.

17. **Longitudinal design is like**
    a. A repeated measures design.
    b. An independent groups design.
    c. A matched participant design.
    d. Counterbalancing.

18. **Which of the following is a non-experimental research method?**
    a. Naturalistic observation.
    b. Interview.
    c. Investigation using correlational analysis.
    d. All of the above.

19. **Which method makes it easier to obtain data from a large sample?**
    a. Experiment.
    b. Questionnaire.
    c. Naturalistic observation.
    d. All of the above.

20. **Which of the following has an IV and a DV?**
    a. Experiment.
    b. Questionnaire.
    c. Naturalistic observation.
    d. Investigation using a correlational analysis.

A key to chapter 5

For each OCR practical activity this chapter provides:

1. Some ideas of what you can do
2. Tips on how to fill out the **PRACTICAL INVESTIGATIONS FOLDER**, including a model* exemplar for the activity.
3. A template for the **BLUE PETER FOLDER**, with tips on filling this in and a model* exemplar.
4. A set of possible exam questions for the activity, with some examiner's tips.
5. Some model* student answers to exam questions for the activity, with examiner's comments.

A model exemplar is an answer that would get full marks. However, it is not the only possible way to get full marks: it is simply one possible answer that is good enough for full mark

COURSEWORK

You must prepare a PRACTICAL INVESTIGATIONS FOLDER containing details of four activities conducted by yourself:

OCR Practical Activity A: Questions, self-reports and questionnaires.

OCR Practical Activity B: An observation.

OCR Practical Activity C: Collection of data to investigate the difference between two conditions.

OCR Practical Activity D: Collection of data involving two independent measures and analysed using a test of correlation.

Your knowledge and understanding of these activities is examined in the PSYCHOLOGICAL INVESTIGATIONS EXAM, a one-hour exam.

PRACTICAL INVESTIGATIONS FOLDER

The examiner will not mark your **PRACTICAL INVESTIGATIONS FOLDER**. But this does not mean that it is not important!!! It is important because a significant number of questions in your examination will involve you copying from the folder. If your folder is incomplete or lacking in detail, you will lose precious marks!

Important! There are some things which you're not allowed write about in your folder. These are:

- Ethical issues.
- The validity and reliability of measurements.
- Alternative ways of measuring the variables.
- The weaknesses in the methodology and ways of reducing them.
- The advantages and disadvantages of each method/design.

This is because you have to take your **PRACTICAL INVESTIGATIONS FOLDER** into the examination, and it gets sent off to the exam board. Therefore, if you write about any of these things, you may be accused of cheating!

However, you need to know about the issues listed above because exam questions are asked about these (see the blue questions). To help you prepare for the blue questions we have drafted a **BLUE PETER FOLDER** (see www.nelsonthornes.com/researchmethods) which you cannot take into the exam but you can revise for the exam beforehand using this **BLUE PETER FOLDER** (ones you prepared earlier).

It is allowable to do the same thing twice (e.g. use daily hassles for OCR Activity A and D) but students who do this often get confused between the two activities and come unstuck in the exam.

There is no requirement in the specification that says the booklet must be all the candidate's own work. But the more work a candidate puts into it, the better they will understand the project and be able to answer exam questions on it.

HEALTH WARNING You will see this sign in parts of this chapter. It is a **HEALTH WARNING**

If you wish to pass your exams do not copy the material in this book. Your teachers and, more importantly, your examiners will know you have copied and you will get zero marks.

The PSYCHOLOGICAL INVESTIGATIONS EXAM consists of three kinds of questions:

- Questions which require you to copy out of your practical investigations folder

  We have placed these questions on a green background.

Usually, about a third or a half of the examination questions involve simply copying from your **PRACTICAL INVESTIGATIONS FOLDER**. This means you can get up to 50% of the paper's marks just by making sure your booklet is completely perfect, detailed and wonderful!

- Questions which ask you about your activity but do not involving copying from the folder

  We have placed these questions on a blue background.

These questions may be about problems or weaknesses, or different ways of conducting the activity. It is important to think about these things before the examination (rather than in the examination). You can prepare for these questions by filling in the **BLUE PETER FOLDER** and also by practicing the blue questions.

- Questions which ask you about general methodological issues

  We have placed these questions on a purple background.

These questions test your understanding of research methods. You can practice these by trying to answer the purple questions and by doing the Multiple Choice Questions at the end of each chapter in Part 1 of this book.

The practical investigations folder and psychological investigations exam

Contents

OCR Practical Activity A

The practical investigations folder

On the left hand side of this spread you are shown how to fill in your folder for Activity A. The form produced by the board contains the titles (shown in black). Examiner's guidance is given in green.

On the right hand side of this spread there is a *model* folder. You will use these answers for the green questions (see page 70) when you sit your exam.

Guidance for filling in Practical Investigations Folder is given below.

Activity A: Questions, self-reports and questionnaires

State the aim of this activity.

There is no requirement for a hypothesis here. A clearly stated aim is fine. It is a good idea to say 'My aim was to find out… using a questionnaire.'

Although it is not necessary for this activity, it can make your questionnaire and investigation more meaningful to look for a difference, for example between males and females or students and teachers, rather than just investigating something without looking for a difference.

Give examples of the questions used, including any rating scales etc.

State how many questions there were in your interview or questionnaire.

It is best to include two or three examples of questions and the options for response e.g. Yes/No; Likert scale etc.

Then, explain how you arrived at a score for each participant's questionnaire. For example, did you just have to count up all the yes's? Or did each a= 3 points, b= 2 points, c = 1 point and so on. Perhaps there were different groups of questions or subscales?

Finally, explain how you interpreted the overall score, or what each score meant. For example, 'a score of 15+ means very stressed out, 10–14 means moderately stressed out…' and so on.

Give details of sample.

Make sure you include:
- Type of sampling method. This will probably be opportunity sample (participants easily available to you), but may also be a quota sample (an opportunity sample, but you decide to have, for example, equal numbers of certain groups such as equal numbers of males and females).
- Number of participants
- Number of males and females
- Age range of participants
- Where you found or approached your participants
- The target (parent) population i.e. who you can generalise to.

Outline the procedure you used for collecting data.

Your procedure needs to be in as much detail as possible. The idea is that anyone could read this procedure and then copy (replicate) your investigation identically. Therefore, you should include:
- How you developed your questionnaire or interview questions. For example, did you use a pre-existing questionnaire? Did you adapt a pre-existing questionnaire? Did you create all the questions yourself?
- Where and when you approached your participants as well as where they actually completed the questionnaire.
- Gaining participants' consent.
- Instructions you gave them for completing the questionnaire or taking part in the interview.
- How you administered your questions e.g. did you read them out and note down the participants' responses; or did you give them a ready-made questionnaire?
- If you gave participants an unlimited amount of time or a time limit to complete the questionnaire.
- Details of any debrief you administered.
- Any details of how you ensured their confidentiality.

Use this space for a summary of your results.

Hopefully, you have gained some quantitative data. This is preferable as it is often easier to summarise. For quantitative data, you could include:
- Table of measures of central tendency and dispersion
- Bar chart of mean score(s)
- Verbal summary of results, i.e. 'looking at the bar chart I can see that….'

NB THERE IS NO REQUIREMENT FOR A STATISTICAL TEST FOR THIS ACTIVITY.

State the conclusions which you drew from your findings.

Try to state two conclusions* about your results. These could refer to:
- Your overall findings (e.g. we found that on the whole people were classed as very high sensation seekers)
- Any patterns in the results e.g. differences between males and females
- Any questions which produced consistently similar responses (e.g. Nearly everyone i.e. 19/20 reported that they 'got bored with seeing the same old faces' – Item 15.)

* Read about the difference between findings and conclusions on page 18

HEALTH WARNING

Activity A: Questions, self-reports and questionnaires

State the aim of this activity.

My aim was to see whether males or females experience more disgust, using a computer-based questionnaire.

Give examples of the questions used, including any rating scales etc.

There were 20 questions altogether. There were 19 in section 1 using a Likert type scale, asking questions about a photograph of a different object, animal or person; and just 1 question in section 2 (multiple choice).

Examples of Section 1 questions:

1. How would you feel about touching …. picture of caterpillars?

☐ ☐ ☐ ☐ ☐
not at all   very
disgusted   disgusted

2. How would you feel about touching …. picture of bad burn on leg?

☐ ☐ ☐ ☐ ☐
not at all   very
disgusted   disgusted

Example of Section 2 questions:

Which of these people's toothbrushes would you LEAST like to use? (choose one)

   (i) your partner

   (ii) your brother or sister nearest in age

   (iii) your best friend

   (iv) your boss

   (v) your postman

   (vi) the weatherman/girl

The score was totalled up from section 1 by giving 1 point to each "not at all disgusted" response, 2 points to the next box etc. and 5 points for each "very disgusted" response.

The total possible score was: 95

Overall scores were interpreted as:

85-95 – easily disgusted

70-84 – quite easily disgusted

55-69 – normal disgust

40-54 – not easily disgusted

0-39 – rarely disgusted.

Give details of sample.

I used a quota sample of 10 males and 10 females, aged between 16 and 18 years old. All were known to me personally at my college and I approached them to take part during free lessons in the library or common room. Therefore, the target population is sixth formers at my school in Newcastle.

Outline the procedure you used for collecting data.

I decided to use a pre-existing web questionnaire on disgust which has been developed by Dr Valerie Curtis from the London School of Hygiene and Tropical Medicine. I did not alter the questionnaire as it was web-based and can be found at:

http://www.bbc.co.uk/science/humanbody/mind/surveys/disgust/index.shtml

I approached a participant in the library or common room at college. I asked for their consent to take part in a survey on "Disgust" and warned them that there were one or two pictures involved which they may find disgusting. All participants approached happily agreed to take part. I then showed them to a computer in the college's computer room and loaded the web page and asked them to work through the questions online, taking as much time as they wished. Meanwhile, I made myself busy with paperwork so they would not feel inhibited by my presence. When they had finished the survey, I asked if I could look at the results. All participants consented. I noted down their numerical responses (1-5) for all the 19 questions in section 1, as well as their response for the toothbrush question (Q20). Fortunately, the website gives a debrief about the survey. I also told each participant that I was interested in finding out whether there is a difference in how easily disgusted males and females are. I reassured them that their responses would be kept confidential and thanked them for their time. All the data was collected between 10.00 am and 4 pm in the second week of November.

Use this space for a summary of your results.

Table showing measures of central tendency and dispersion for scores on disgust survey comparing males and females.

	Male disgust scores	Female disgust scores
Mean	58.7	61.2
Median	59.5	59
Mode	None	58
Range	24	25

Bar chart showing mean male and female scores on the disgust survey

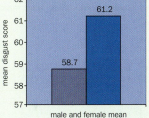

Looking at the bar chart I can see that there is not much difference between the male and female mean disgust scores, but that the males have scored on average, slightly lower (58.7 compared to 61.2), indicating that males get slightly less disgusted than females.

For section 2 of the test ("whose toothbrush would you least like to use"), results were very similar between the two sexes (see bar chart below).

Bar chart showing least preferred toothbrush sharer with least preferred person being the postman!

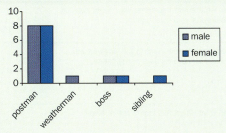

State the conclusions which you drew from your findings.

I can conclude that:

* Females are very slightly more easily disgusted than males

* People are least likely to want to use the postman's toothbrush.

OCR Practical Activity A

The Blue Peter folder

Some of the questions in the exam involve copying from your PRACTICAL INVESTIGATIONS FOLDER; other questions involve more than just copying. It is more than a good idea to consider such possible questions before you are sitting at your little examination desk. Consider them now! A good idea is to create a BLUE PETER FOLDER (one that I prepared earlier) to write down all your ideas about improvements to each investigation, their effects upon results, key definitions and concepts etc. There is a blank version of the BLUE PETER FOLDER on the website (see www.nelsonthornes.com/researchmethods).This folder will get you ready for the blue questions (see page 70) so that you will have these answers 'up your sleeve' (so to speak) when you sit your exam.

Describe **one** weakness in the way that your questionnaire was devised.	Possibilities to think about: • Are any of the questions ambiguous? • Are any of the questions unethical e.g. too personal or socially sensitive? • Are any of the questions aimed at the wrong sort of respondents e.g. an older age group? • Are there too many questions? • Is the questionnaire too difficult to score? • Was the aim of the questionnaire too obvious, causing demand characteristics? You also need to explain why this is a weakness, i.e. what problems did this create?
Suggest an alternative scoring or rating system to the one you used.	Other possible scoring systems: • Yes vs No – e.g. just score all the Yes's. • **Likert scale:** e.g 7 point scale, where 1 = Strongly disagree and 7 = Strongly agree. • Also consider how it will effect how you score your questionnaire overall and interpret those scores.
What effect this alternative scoring or rating system would have on your results?	Consider whether it would: • Create more or less honest responses? • Force people to make more definite answers? • Create a more noticeable difference between the groups of people you might be comparing?
Describe **one** strength in the way that you selected your sample.	Consider: • Size of sample – perhaps you had a large sample. • If participants volunteered they should be keen and so take the task seriously and answer questions relatively truthfully. • If you had a good range of ages or good mix of gender.
Describe **one** weakness in the way that you selected your sample.	Consider: • If you had a small sample e.g. less than 10. • If you only selected a very limited type of sample (e.g. one kind of student, such as only Psychology students) and so it is not representative of your target population (sixth form students). • If it was heavily weighted towards one gender only, such as 17 females and 3 males.
Describe **one** improvement to the way that you selected your sample.	Depends upon what you have identified above, but describe your improvement clearly and in detail.
Describe **one** weakness in the way that you collected data for this investigation.	Try to avoid sampling. Think instead about something more specific to your study. This will make your answer more contextualized. • How you administered your questionnaire e.g. did you give enough time? • Where you administered your questionnaire – was it too noisy, were others watching? • Whether participants felt their answers were confidential enough.
Suggest another way of collecting data for this investigation.	This could be another method e.g. observation, experiment etc., that is looking at the same behaviour or aspect of psychology. Make sure you give enough detail for the examiner to really understand.
Explain what effect this 'other way' might have on the findings of your investigation.	Consider: • More or less **validity / ecological validity**? • More or less **demand characteristics**?
Suggest **one** improvement to the way that you collected your data for your investigation.	Could consider: • Where you collected your data. • How you administered your questions – on paper, verbally, on a computer. You need to explain why this would be an improvement i.e. what was the problem you had, why this needs some improvement, and how your suggestion achieves this.
Explain what effect this improvement might have on your results.	Consider: • More or less validity / ecological validity?? More demand characteristics? • Difference in your overall results?
Suggest **one** way you could test the validity of your self-report measure.	Good idea to talk about **concurrent validity** i.e. comparing the results of your questionnaire with the results from the same participants on another questionnaire also claiming to measure the same thing. Make sure you clearly relate the answer to your self report measure.
Suggest **one** way you could test the reliability of your self-report measure.	Good idea to talk about **external reliability** i.e. if you conducted the same questionnaire on the same participants at a later date then you should get very similar results for each participant, i.e. consistency over time. Make sure you clearly relate the answer to your self-report measure.
Explain **one** ethical issue you had to consider when conducting your investigation.	Possibilities: • Whether questions are socially sensitive, embarrassing or disturbing. • **Confidentiality** of the participants' responses. • Gaining **informed consent**, which might create more demand characteristics.

PRACTICAL INVESTIGATIONS

Describe **one** weakness in the way that your questionnaire was devised.

Level of disgust was measured on a five-point scale, where 1 = not at all disgusted and 5 = very disgusted. This meant that sometimes people put the middle answer (option 3) rather than making a more definite choice.

Suggest an alternative scoring or rating system to the one you used.

Instead of using a Likert scale, I could have used just a Yes or No response: "do you find this picture disgusting, Yes or no?" Participants would just circle the one that most applied to them. I would give a point for each yes, to a maximum of 19. 17+ would mean easily disgusted, 14-18 quite easily disgusted and so on.

What effect would this alternative scoring or rating system have on your results?

This would probably make the results less valid. Yes/no gives less choice to participants and they end up being forced into saying "Yes it is disgusting", when they really want to say "Yes, it's just a bit disgusting". However, it might stop people putting down the middle response all the time. Therefore I might see a greater difference between males and females as people won't be able to 'sit on the fence'.

Describe **one** strength in the way that you selected your sample.

It was a quota sample. This meant that there was an even number of males and females (i.e. 10 of each) as so it allowed for better comparison between the males and females' level of disgust because they were identical amounts of each.

Describe **one** weakness in the way that you selected your sample.

One problem was that I approached only people I knew, generally because we are in the same classes together. This means that this sample was not representative of all the sixth formers in my college because certain kinds of sixth formers were not approached. For example, none of my sample were studying Physics or Chemistry A levels, and none of them were studying Vocational A levels such as Leisure and Recreation. Therefore my sample is not representative of all sixth formers at my college.

Describe **one** improvement to the way that you selected your sample.

I could have chosen a random sampling method for my target population (i.e. sixth formers at my college). This would mean that, rather than just approach people who were convenient, I would put all sixth formers' names into a hat and pick out the first 20 names. So each student would have an equal chance of taking part in the study & so I would probably have a more representative sample with students from a wider range of subject areas.

Describe **one** weakness in the way that you collected data for this investigation

One problem was that many of the participants knew each other and so discussed and talked about the questionnaire to other participants before I had collected their data. This may have affected the way some people answered their questions as they had expectations. For example, one participant remarked to another about how revolting such and such a picture was. When this second participant came to fill in the questionnaire, they may have felt that they should give that picture a high disgust rating, even if they personally did not. This would have affected the validity of their own answer.

Suggest another way of collecting data for this investigation.

Another way of collecting data about male and female differences in disgust would be to do a kind of controlled observation. I could set up some test tubes with different smells that may provoke disgust and get people to smell them. For example, I could have a tube of rotten eggs smell (sulphur), a tube of urine-like smell (ammonia) and so on. Some tubes could have more neutral or non-disgusting smells such as citrus. As each participant smells each smell, an observer could rate their behaviour according to how much disgust is shown e.g. pulling faces, making disgust noises and so on.

Explain what effect this "other way" might have on the findings of your investigation.

This could make the results more valid. This is because sometimes when people are just answering questions (self-report) they may not tell the truth because they are not in that actual situation, or because they want to be seen in a certain way (social desirability bias). But in this new study, it is difficult to not tell the truth as 'actions speak louder than words'. It is difficult to pretend that you find a smell ok when really you feel disgusted.

Suggest **one** improvement to the way that you collected your data.

I could ask people to take part in the questionnaire much more individually, rather than as a group of friends in the library. In other words, each participant would not know other participants who were taking part. This would have prevented participants discussing the nature of the pictures and how disgusting or not disgusting they were before they had even taken the test.

Explain what effect this improvement might have on your results.

This would prevent people discussing the questionnaire before they had taken it themselves. This would mean that they would have no expectation about how disgusting a certain picture might be, or how they should respond. It would also prevent some exaggerating disgust because someone had said it was or was not disgusting. So people would answer more honestly, increasing the validity of their responses.

Suggest **one** way you could test the validity of your questionnaire.

I could find another questionnaire that measures disgust. I could then test each of the participants again on this second questionnaire. If my questionnaire is valid, then participants' disgust scores should be similar on each of the questionnaires. I could correlate the results to confirm this and would expect to find a positive correlation. This is called concurrent validity.

Suggest **one** way you could test the reliability of your self-report measure.

I could ask people to do the same questionnaire on disgust again one month later. I would then correlate their scores on their first test with their scores on the second test. If the questionnaire is reliable, I would expect a strong positive correlation between disgust scores. This is test-retest method.

Explain **one** ethical issue you had to consider when conducting your investigation.

One issue was harm. Some of the pictures were really a bit disgusting (although they only had to look at them for a short period), such as the one with maggots in a person's gums. Also, if someone was squeamish of blood, they may not have liked the one of the infected burn. However, when I approached people to take part and asked for consent, I did warn them that it included one or two questions which they may find disgusting. If they had felt this might be a problem, they would have been able to decline to take part. But nobody did.

OCR Practical Activity A

Sample exam questions

See page 62 for an explanation of these questions.

Note that the questions provided here do not represent all the questions that may ever be asked but they do cover most of the possibilities.

*These are the sorts of questions which candidates find the most challenging. Practise the answers to these before the examination. Then you will be well prepared! You can do this by filling in the **BLUE PETER FOLDER**.*

GREEN QUESTIONS: Examples of questions asking you to copy out of your practical investigation folder.

1. Outline the aim of your activity. [2]

2. Describe your questionnaire or interview. [3]

3. Give an example of **one** of your questions. [2]

4. Describe the scoring system or rating scale that you used. [3]

5. Describe the sample that you used for this activity. [3]

6. Describe the sampling method that you used for this activity. [2]

7. Outline the procedure that you used for collecting your self-report data. [3]

8. Describe how you presented your questionnaire. [2]

9. Outline the results of your questionnaire. [3]

10. Outline **two** of your findings. [2]

11. Outline **one** conclusion that you made. [2]

PURPLE QUESTIONS: Examples of questions about self-report in general.

1. Describe **two** advantages of self-report measures. [4]

2. Describe **two** disadvantages of self-report measures. [4]

3. Describe what psychologists mean by the term reliability. [2]

4. Describe what psychologists mean by the term validity. [2]

BLUE QUESTIONS: examples of questions about your activity but not involving copying from the folder.

1. Describe **one** weakness in the way that your questionnaire was devised. [3]

2. (a) Suggest an alternative scoring or rating system to the one you used. [3]

   (b) Outline what effect this alternative may have on your results. [3]

3. Describe **one** strength in the way you selected your sample for your investigation. [3]

4. (a) Describe **one** weakness in the way you selected your sample for your investigation. [3]

   (b) Describe **one** improvement to the way you selected your sample for your investigation. [3]

5. Describe **one** weakness in the way that you collected your data for your investigation. [3]

6. (a) Suggest another way of collecting data for this investigation. [3]

   (b) Explain what effect this might have on the findings of your investigation. [3]

7. (a) Suggest **two** improvements to the way that you collected your data for your investigation. [6]

   (b) Explain the effect that **one** of these improvements would have on your results. [3]

8. (a) Suggest **one** change to the way that you collected your data for your investigation. [3]

   (b) Explain what effect this improvement may have on the validity of your results. [3]

9. Suggest **one** way you could test the validity of your questionnaire. [4]

10. Suggest **one** way you could test the reliability of your questionnaire. [4]

11. Explain **one** ethical issue you had to consider when conducting your study. [3]

Can you identify which questions on the facing page are green questions, blue questions and purple questions?

Model answers to exam questions

1. (a) Outline the aim of your investigation. [2]
My aim was to see whether males or females experience more disgust, using a computer-based questionnaire.

(b) Suggest another way of collecting data for your investigation. [3]
Another way of collecting data about male and female differences in disgust would be to do a kind of controlled observation. I could set up some test tubes with different smells that may provoke disgust and get people to smell them. For example, I could have a tube of rotten eggs smell (sulphur), a tube of urine-like smell (ammonia) and so on. Some tubes could have more neutral or non-disgusting smells such as citrus. As each participant smells each smell, an observer could rate their behaviour according to how much disgust is shown e.g. pulling faces, making disgust noises and so on.

(c) Explain what effect this change may have on the results of your investigation. [3]
This could make the results more valid. This is because sometimes when people are just answering questions (self-report) they may not tell the truth because they are not in that actual situation, or because they want to be seen in a certain way (social desirability bias). But in this new study, it is difficult to not tell the truth as "actions speak louder than words". It is difficult to pretend that you find a smell ok when really you feel disgusted.

2. (a) Describe the scoring or rating scale that you used. [3]
I used a Likert scale with 5 points on each of the 19 questions, e.g.:

1. How would you feel about touching....picture of caterpillars

not at all disgusted ☐ ☐ ☐ ☐ ☐ very disgusted

The score was totalled up from section 1 by giving 1 point to each "not at all disgusted" response, 2 points to the next box etc. and 5 points for each "very disgusted" response to a total out of a maximum of 95 points. Overall scores were interpreted as: 85-95 – easily disgusted; 70-84 quite easily disgusted; 55-69 normal disgust; 40-54 not easily disgusted; 0-39 rarely disgusted.

(b) Suggest an alternative rating or scoring system to the one you used. [3]
Instead of using a Likert scale, I could have used just a Yes or No response: "do you find this picture disgusting, Yes or No?" Participants would just circle the one that most applied to them. I would give a point for each Yes, to a maximum of 19. 17+ would mean easily disgusted, 14-18 quite easily disgusted and so on.

(c) Explain what effect this alternative would have on your results. [3]
This would probably make the results less valid. Yes/No gives less choice to participants and they end up being forced into saying Yes, when they really want to say "Yes just a bit". However, it might stop people putting down the middle response all the time. Therefore I might see a greater difference between males and females as people won't be able to 'sit on the fence'.

3. (a) Briefly outline what psychologists mean by the term reliability. [2]
Reliability means consistency. External reliability means consistency over time. So if a questionnaire is repeated at a later date on the same people, they should get pretty much the same results.

(b) Explain how you could test the reliability of your self-report measure. [4]
I could ask people to do the same questionnaire again one month later. I would then correlate their scores on their first test with their scores on the second test. If the questionnaire is reliable, I would expect a strong positive correlation between disgust scores.

4. Suggest *one* problem in the way that you conducted your investigation. [3]
One problem was ethics. Some of the pictures were really a bit disgusting (although they only had to look at them for a short period), such as the one with maggots in a person's gums. Also, if someone was squeamish of blood, they may not have liked the one of the infected burn. I should have checked out people's squeamishness or if they had a phobia of blood before showing them pictures just to make sure I would not offend anyone (psychological harm).

Examiner's comments

1. (a) This is perfectly fine for two marks – two fairly easy marks!

1. (b) This can seem like a daunting question. It asks for 'another way', allowing all sorts of possibilities. The candidate could have simply opted for a variation on their questionnaire or an **interview** (keeping essentially the same **research method**) but this candidate has opted for a different method entirely, to good effect. This seems a well thought-through response, presenting a plausible alternative to collect data about disgust responses.

1. (c) Again, this is quite well answered, and one suspects that some forethought has gone into this (i.e. he has worked through BLUE QUESTIONS before the exam.) This would get 3 marks as it does really follow through the change and its impact on results.

2. (a) This is a GREEN QUESTION – straight forward copying from the booklet. No memory is required. Just a completed booklet.

2. (b) This is a likely alternative – switch Likert for another closed answer response. This would gain full marks because the candidate has contextualised their response in terms of their study and explained it clearly and coherently, following through with the consequences on the overall interpretation of the scores.

2. (c) There is a good appreciation here of how forced choice answers (Yes vs No) can work to the questioner's advantage. The candidate manages to contextualise their response within their own study, but this could be more effective by talking more specifically about differences in disgust scores for males and females. Therefore they would receive 2/3.

3. (a) Just saying consistency would get 1 mark. The candidate clearly understands the concept of external reliability, or test-retest.

3. (b) This question requires the candidate to contextualise their answer in terms of their own study, which this candidate has succeeded in doing by reference to disgust scores. A common mistake with test-retest is that candidates sometimes fail to make it clear that the retest should be performed on the same, original participants.

4. This is a nice response because the problem is so clearly related to issues around this specific investigation. The candidate has not described the ubiquitous problem of 'not enough participants', and the problem is clearly described and explained. It actually is easier (and gets more marks!) for candidates to talk in more detail about a 'real' problem rather than 'any old problem I can come up with' such as sampling.

OCR Practical Activity B

The practical investigations folder

On the left hand side of this spread you are shown how to fill in your folder for Activity B. The form produced by the board contains the titles (shown in black). Examiner's guidance for each title is given in green.

On the right hand side of this spread there is a *model* folder. You will use these answers for the green questions (see page 78) when you sit your exam.

Guidance for filling in Practical Investigations Folder is given below.

Activity B: An Observation

State the aim of this activity.

All you need here is the aim and not a complete hypothesis, though it is still important to phrase your aim clearly.

Describe the categories of behaviour that you observed and the rating or coding system that you used.

Here you need to describe, in detailed fashion, the coding system or behaviour checklist or rating scale which you used for each of your categories of behaviour. In order to achieve this:

- State your categories of behaviour.
- Draw an 'empty' or demonstration tally chart, e.g. as shown below.

	Healthy food	Unhealthy food
Male	IIII	IIII
Female	II	II

- Explain how observed behaviours were categorized into your above-named categories.

The guiding principle here is replication; i.e. should another person wish to conduct a similar observation, they should be able to adopt exactly the same coding system without having any queries about it.

Give details of the sample that you observed.

Describe:

- The sampling method which you used; probably an opportunity sample or it might be a volunteer (self-selecting) sample i.e. a sample that is selected on the basis of their own action by walking though the sampling point
- Number of participants
- Age range of participants. If you have conducted your observation with sixth form students, you can be quite precise here. However, if you have conducted your study in the town centre or on a bus, you can give an approximate age range.
- Number of males compared to number of females
- Where you found your participants
- The target (parent) population.

Outline the procedure that you followed for your observation.

Again, the guiding principle here is replication i.e. any reader of this procedure should be able to copy your observational study exactly should they wish to. Don't forget to include:

- When your observation took place i.e. time of day as well as date; and for how long
- Where your observation took place
- Whether your participants knew they were being observed or not
- The number of observers
- How many observers recorded the behaviour.

Describe any other details of the procedure that are relevant!

Summarise your findings.

How you summarise your data depends upon how you have coded behaviour. Probably, you have put people and their behaviour into categories; in which case you will need:

- A summary table or tables showing raw frequencies and percentages of behaviours observed, for example:

Table showing numbers (frequency) of males and female who bought healthy or unhealthy food in the college cafeteria

	Healthy food	Unhealthy food
Male	12	28
Female	20	17

Table showing percentages of males and percentages of females buying healthy or unhealthy food in the college cafeteria.

	Healthy food	Unhealthy food
Male	30% of males	60% of males
Female	54% of females	46% of females

- Either a pie chart (or perhaps a pair of pie charts) showing percentages, or a bar chart
- A brief written description of the results: 'Looking at the table I can see that…'.

NB If you have conducted an observation where you have rated people (i.e. assigned a score to each person), then it is possible to calculate means etc.

NB In this activity, there is no requirement for you to do a statistical test.

Give your conclusions.

Say what your study seems to show. It is a good idea to try to write about two conclusions.

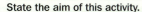

Activity B: An Observation

State the aim of this activity.

The aim of this activity is to see whether there is a difference in female and male students on-task and off-task behaviour in a Psychology class.

Describe the categories of behaviour that you observed and the rating or coding system that you used.

My categories of behaviour were male: on-task, male: off-task, female: on-task, female: off-task, as observed at three sampling points throughout the lesson.

Time of sample	9.05 am		9.35 am		10.05 am	
	On-task	Off-task	On-task	Off-task	On-task	Off-task
Male	卌 I	III	III	卌 I	III	卌 I
Female	卌 II	III	卌 IIII	I	卌 I	IIII

On-task behaviour was coded as:
• Writing notes
• Listening to teacher
• Looking at board or screen
• Answering teacher's questions
• Doing task teacher had set
• Talking to neighbour about psychology
• Asking teacher relevant question.

Off-task behaviour was coded as:
• Playing with mobile phone
• Doodling
• Looking out of the window
• Looking as if day-dreaming.
• Asking teacher non-relevant question.
• Talking to friend about topic not related to lesson

Give details of the sample that you observed.

This was an opportunity sample of 20 AS psychology students in my class at the time of the observation, in a 9am to 10.10 am class on 1st November. There were 9 males and 11 females in the class, aged between 16 years old and 18 years old. Therefore the target population is Psychology AS students at my sixth form college.

Outline the procedure that you followed for your observation.

I asked my teacher for consent to conduct the observation in the class. I decided to do time sampling at three points throughout the 9 am – 10.10 am lesson, rather than just a one-off observation. I decided to observe at 9.05am (near the beginning of the lesson, when everyone should have arrived and the lesson is underway), 9.35 am (in the middle of the lesson), and 10.05 (near the end of the lesson where some people may have decided to "switch off" early).

At each of the three sampling points, I looked around the room at each student in turn and put a tally on my tally chart depending on whether the student was male or female and whether their behaviour could be categorized as on-task or off-task according to the coding scheme. (I did not code my own behaviour.) I was sitting near the front of the classroom and the seats were arranged in a horseshoe shape, so I could see all the other students' faces clearly. I was the only observer.

At the end of the lesson, I thanked my teacher and showed him my tally chart.

Summarise your findings.

Table showing frequencies of male and female on- and off- task behaviour in a psychology class

Time of sample	9.05 am		9.35 am		10.05 am	
	On-task	Off-task	On-task	Off-task	On-task	Off-task
Male	6	3	3	6	3	6
Female	7	3	9	1	6	4

Table showing overall percentages of on- and off-task behaviour for males and females in a psychology class

	% on-task by gender	% off-task by gender
Male	44%	56%
Female	73%	27%

Bar chart: % male and female on- and off- task behaviour in Psychology lesson

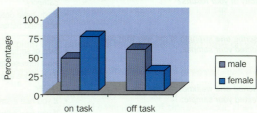

Looking at the results and graph I can see that males are more likely to be off-task than on-task.

Give your conclusions.

Males are more off-task than on-task. Also, males are more off-task than females; who are generally more likely to be on-task than off-task in psychology lessons. Additionally, all students are more off-task at the end of the lesson than at the beginning or in the middle.

HEALTH WARNING

OCR Practical Activity B

Sample exam questions

See page 62 for an explanation of these questions.

Note that the questions provided here do not represent all the questions that may ever be asked but they do cover most of the possibilities.

PRACTICAL INVESTIGATIONS

These blue questions are the sort of questions which candidates find the most challenging. Practise the answers to these before the examination. Then you will be well prepared! You can do this by filling in the **BLUE PETER FOLDER**.

GREEN QUESTIONS: Examples of questions asking you to copy out of your practical investigation folder.

1. Outline the aim of your observation. [2]

2. Describe the categories of behaviour that you observed and the rating or coding scheme. [4]

3. Describe the sample that you used for this activity. [3]

4. Describe the sampling method that you used for this activity. [3]

5. Describe the procedure that you followed for your observation. [4]

6. Outline **two** of your findings from your observation. [4]

7. Describe **one** conclusion that can be drawn from your results. [2]

PURPLE QUESTIONS Examples of questions about observational methods and techniques in general.

1. Describe **one** advantage of observational research. [3]

2. Describe **one** disadvantage of observational research. [3]

3. Describe what is meant by the term reliability. [2]

4. Describe what is meant by the term validity. [2]

5. A researcher wishes to observe doctor–patient interactions in a hospital.

    (a) Suggest **two** categories of behaviour the researcher may observe. [4]

    (b) Describe **one** ethical issue the researcher should consider before conducting this observation. [2]

BLUE QUESTIONS: examples of questions about your activity but not involving copying from the folder.

1. Describe **one** weakness in the way you categorised the behaviour you were observing. [3]

2. (a) Suggest an alternative way of categorizing the behaviour you were observing. [3]

    (b) Explain what effect this may have on the validity. Does this just refer to ecological validity? [3]

3. Describe **one** weakness in the way that you conducted your observation. [3]

4. Describe **one** weakness in the way that you selected your sample for your observation. [2]

5. (a) Outline **one** ethical problem you considered when you planned your study. [2]

    (b) Explain how you overcame this ethical problem. [3]

6. Suggest how the reliability of your observation could be improved.

7. (a) Describe **one** improvement to your observation. [3]

    (b) Explain what effect this improvement might have on your results. [3]

Can you identify which questions on the facing page are green questions, blue questions and purple questions?

OCR Practical Activity B

Model answer questions

1. (a) Describe *one* weakness in the way you categorized the behaviour you observed. [3]

One problem was that I only had two main categories of behaviour: on-task and off-task. This was a problem because on some occasions when I was observing students, I could not decide whether they were on- or off- task. For example, some students may be looking at the board, but I was not sure they were necessarily concentrating. Also, sometimes, students were talking to each other when they were supposed to be doing pair-work but I could not hear whether they were talking about the task or about what they did last night. Therefore, I think there were not enough categories to fit all my observations.

(b) Describe *one* way of overcoming this weakness in the way that you categorized the behaviour you observed. [3]

I could have had three categories of behaviour: Firstly, on-task behaviour including writing notes, asking questions, completing task set by teacher; secondly off-task behaviour, including playing with phone, audibly talking on a topic not related to the lesson; thirdly, not possible to determine whether on- or off-task. This third category would include talking to neighbour but when observer is unsure whether it is about a lesson-related topic or not; or looking at the board/teacher but not with a concentrated expression.

2. (a) Outline *one* ethical problem you considered when you planned your study. [2]

One ethical issue I considered was consent. This is a problem because if I asked the students in my class for consent, they may have behaved differently due to the fact they know they are being observed. On the other hand, although my teacher was not being observed directly, it would have been his class and he may not have wished me to investigate this. Thus, I felt consent was an issue.

(b) Explain how you overcame this ethical problem. [3]

I decided to ask my teacher for consent on behalf of the whole class. This meant that, in giving his consent, he could not object to me investigating his class and spending some of the class time 'not doing what I was supposed to'; also, because the students are in an environment (though not exactly a public place) where they are used to being observed then these observations are now ethical with the teacher's consent.

3 (a) Describe what psychologists mean by the term reliability. [2]

Reliability means consistency. In observations this often means the consistency between two observers' categorisations or ratings when watching the same behaviour i.e. inter-rater reliability.

(b) Suggest how the reliability of your study could be improved. [4]

I could have conducted a pilot study where there were two observers. We could have both sat at different vantage points in the classroom and coded behaviour at the same times. Then, we should have compared our results. If we agreed (e.g. both agreed that student 1 was on-task and so on...), we would have good inter-rater reliability. However, if we had not agreed then this would be a good chance to improve the reliability between us by refining and clarifying the categories of behaviour.

4. (a) Describe *one* improvement to your observation. [3]

I could have observed students at more points throughout the lesson. I watched them three times – 5 mins into the beginning, the middle and then 5 mins before the end. But because the lesson is quite long (1 hour and 10 minutes), then I did not really get to observe enough of how on- and off-task people were during the main part of the lesson i.e. the bit that really counts. Therefore, I should have sampled students' behaviour every 10 minutes i.e. 9.05, 9.15, 9.25, 9.35 etc until 10.05, making seven observations altogether instead of just three.

4. (b) Explain what effect this improvement would have on the results. [3]

This will change the results. Informally, I observed that the males had trouble concentrating at the beginning and end of the lesson, but were generally better during the main part of the lesson. Therefore, if I sample more of this behaviour, then it may show that there is not such a great difference between male and female on- and off-task behaviour and that males too spend more time on-task than off-task.

Examiner's comments

1.(a) This is a good answer as it clearly explains a flaw in the categorization of the observed behaviour and the problems that arose out of that. The student could also have said how this problem resulted in putting observed behaviours into incorrect categories.

1.(b) This answer follows on naturally from the part (a). Often candidates do not read all the questions before answering and in such a pair of questions as this one can fall into one of two traps: (1) get to part (b) and realize they do not know how to remedy the weakness they have just written about in part (a), or (2) start writing about how to remedy it in part (a) rather than where it should be in (b). In this case, the material will not receive credit as it is not written under part (b). Remember, each answer is marked independently of another; so each of your answers should be 'stand alone' and not depend on information that you have written down elsewhere.

The candidate here has succeeded in clearly describing the new categories and coding system.

2. (a) Clear explanation of the ethical quandary, very clearly related to the candidates own observational study; more than enough for two marks.

2. (b) Good awareness of the finer points of the guidelines for consent, nicely contextualized.

3. (a) Clear definition. The candidate has chosen to answer this in terms of **inter-rater** reliability; but an answer in terms of could also get two marks.

3. (b) This part of the question requires the candidate to contextualise reliability in his own observation. He achieves this well by referring to the classroom and the coding of on- and off-task.

4. (a) The strength of this candidate's response is that he has identified an improvement which is specifically about his own study, and not a generic improvement e.g. larger number of participants. His improvement is appropriate and well explained.

4. (b) This is a thoughtful response and shows that the candidate clearly understood his original investigation. This response really does answer the question as it deals with results and not just more generic issues like validity or generalisability.

OCR Practical Activity C

The practical investigations folder

On the left hand side of this spread you are shown how to fill in your folder for Activity C. The form produced by the board contains the titles (shown in black). Examiner's guidance is given for each title in green.

On the right hand side of this spread there is a *model folder*. You will use these answers for the green questions (see page 86) when you sit your exam.

Guidance for filling in Practical Investigations Folder is given below.

Activity C: Collection of data to investigate the difference between two conditions

State the hypothesis and null hypothesis for this activity.

Both hypotheses need to be included with both in full detail. Make sure you operationalise your DV and say how your IV will be implemented. Say whether your research hypothesis (H_1) is one or two tailed.

Identify the variables.

Identify the IV. Identify the two conditions. Identify the DV. Explain exactly how the DV is measured.

Describe the two conditions.

Clearly describe the two conditions, including references to any materials used, word lists presented etc. that form part of these two conditions.

Give details of the sample that you used for your investigation.

You need to include:

- The type of sample used (probably opportunity sample).
- The number of participants.
- Age range of participants.
- Number of males and number of females.
- Where they were sourced from (e.g. your psychology class or your friends at college).
- Target (parent) population.

Outline the design/procedure.

- Research design (repeated measures, matched participants, independent measures),
- A step-by-step version of your procedure so that it is replicable, including:
  - Where your experiment was carried out
  - Time of day it was carried out.
  - Details of instructions given to participants.
  - Exact details of tasks participants had to undertake. including a description of any materials used.
  - Any relevant details of time limits participants were given etc.
  - Details of any debrief administered.

Name the statistical test used to analyse the data.

All that is needed here is just the name of the statistical test.

What were the results of your analysis.

You would use the Mann–Whitney or Wilcoxon Test. Here you need to write down the results of the Mann–Whitney or Wilcoxon i.e. the calculated value of U or T. You also need to write the critical value of U or T for your number of participants, and to record the corresponding value of p (see pages 140 and 141 for assistance).

State your conclusions including statements of significance relating to the hypothesis.

Explain the relationship between your calculated value of U or T and how this relates to the critical value and the resulting value of p. Then you can say whether you will accept or reject your null hypothesis.

Use this space to present data using tables, visual displays and verbal summaries.

You ideally need three things here:

1. Table of measures of central tendency and dispersion for the two conditions (i.e. mean, median, mode and range). This table should have a title. Also, you should clearly indicate what the numbers are measuring. (NB you do not need a table of your raw results.)
2. Visual display, probably a bar chart, comparing the mean scores of the two conditions.
3. A verbal summary or description of the data e.g. 'Looking at the graph I can see thait ...; also, interestingly, looking at the range ... I can see that ...'

Use this space to present data using tables, visual displays and verbal summaries.

It is not necessary for the examination to include all your calculations in the booklet. But it is good practice to have a set of raw results.

If you decide to attach it, just get the piece of paper with all the workings on and staple or glue it in, folding it over.

HEALTH WARNING

Activity C: Collection of data to investigate the difference between two conditions

State the hypothesis and null hypothesis for this activity.

H₁ More words are recalled (out of 20) for participants given the cues than participants not given cues. (one tailed)

H₀ There is no difference in the number of words recalled by participants given the cues and those not given the cues.

Identify the variables.

IV: Whether participants are given cues for groups of words or not.

DV: Number of words recalled out of twenty. The twenty words consist of 5 groups of 4 words. (Animals x 4; Furniture x 4; Food x 4; Buildings x 4; Household items x 4).

Describe the two conditions.

In the experimental condition, participants are given 40 seconds to read a list of twenty words, divided into five groups of four with name of each group provided: Buildings: museum, house, library, school (participants asked to memorise the words emboldened). After the distraction task, participants are asked to recall the words and are given the group name cues such as Buildings on a sheet of paper.

In the control condition, everything is the same, but when asked to recall the cues they are not supplied with the group name cues and just supplied with a blank piece of paper.

Give details of the sample that you used for your investigation.

There were 20 participants, selected using an opportunity sampling technique as all were members of my psychology class, 12 were female and 8 were male, all aged between 16 and 17 years old. Therefore, the parent population is psychology students at sixth form college in Cambridgeshire.

Outline the design/procedure.

Each participant was asked to give his/her consent to take part in a study of memory. When consent was gained, participants were all given a list of words consisting of twenty words on a piece of paper. The twenty words had been subdivided into 5 groups of 4 words (Animals, Furniture, Food, Buildings and Household Items). The group word was on the left and the words to be memorized were on the right.

Household Items:	Rug, Television, Cooker, Fridge

E.g:

Participants were given 40 seconds to read through and memorize the words. Then the word lists were removed. Immediately, pps were given a distraction task to ensure we were testing LTM and not STM. The distraction task was 6 sums such as: (4+8)/3= ___ given on another piece of paper. After 30 seconds of doing the distraction task (whether participants had finished all the sums or not), participants were then given a sheet of paper and asked to write down the original twenty words. Participants in the Experimental Condition were given a sheet with the Group Names printed on the left hand side (household items, furniture etc) to act as cues. Participants in the control condition were given a blank piece of paper with no Group Names to act as cues.

Participants were given up to 3 minutes to recall as many words as possible. Participants were allocated to experimental or control group by tossing a coin where head=experimental and tail=control. When this had been collected in, the pps were debriefed and told the purpose of the experiment. This was an independent measures design as each participant only took part in one condition.

Name the statistical test used to analyse data.

Mann–Whitney U test

What were the results of your analysis?

Calculated U = 25.5. Critical U = 27 (n=10,10, p=0.05 one tailed). Therefore p < 0.05 i.e. significant.

State your conclusions including statements of significance relating to the hypothesis.

The calculated U is smaller than the critical value of U, p <0.05. This means that there is less than 5% doubt and more than 95% certainty that the results occurred due to the IV and not due to chance factors. Thus we can reject the null hypothesis and accept H₁: Significantly more words were recalled for participants given the cues than participants not given cues.

Use this space to present data using tables, visual displays and verbal summaries.

	No of words recalled	
	With cues	Without cues
Mean	14.5	10.4
Median	15.5	10.5
Mode	12,15,17	7,10,12
range	9	7

Table showing measures of central tendency and dispersion for number of words recalled in condition given cues compared with condition not given cues

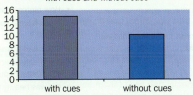

Mean no of words recalled comparing with cues and without cues

Looking at the graph I can see that pps have recalled more words in the "with cues" condition (mean= 14.5) than in the "without condition" (mean = 10.4). Also, looking at the table of data I can see that there is greater dispersion in the with cues condition (range = 9) than in the without cues condition (range = 7). This suggests that the cues have helped pps to recall the words.

The activity reported here is similar to the activity on page 16 – but there are important differences.

OCR Practical Activity C

Sample exam questions

See page 62 for an explanation of these questions.

Note that the questions provided here do not represent all the questions that may ever be asked but they do cover most of the possibilities.

*These blue questions are the sort of questions which candidates find the most challenging. Practise the answers to these before the examination. Then you will be well prepared! You can do this by filling in the **BLUE PETER FOLDER**.*

GREEN QUESTIONS: Examples of questions asking you to copy out of your practical investigation folder.

1. State the null hypothesis for your investigation. [3]
2. State the hypothesis for your investigation. [3]
3. Identify the **two** variables for your investigation. [4]
4. Describe the **two** conditions in this activity. [4]
5. Describe how the dependent variable was measured. [3]
6. Describe the sample that you used for this activity. [3]
7. Describe the sampling method that you used for this activity. [2]
8. Name the experimental design you used for this activity. [2]
9. Describe the procedure that you used for this activity. [4]
10. Sketch a summary of your results in an appropriate visual display. [3]
11. Draw a summary table of your results. [3]
12. Describe **two** findings from your investigation. [4]
13. Name the statistical test you used to analyse your data. [1]
14. (a) Outline the conclusion you reached in relation to your null hypothesis. [3]
    (b) Explain how you reached that conclusion. [3]

BLUE QUESTIONS: examples of questions about your activity but not involving copying from the folder.

1. Describe **one** strength in the way that you conducted your investigation. [3]
2. Describe **one** weakness in the way that you conducted your investigation. [3]
3. Describe **one** weakness in the way that you selected your sample. [3]
4. Describe **one** alternative way of selecting your sample. [3]
5. (a) Describe an alternative way of measuring your dependent variable. [3]
   (b) Explain what effect this alternative would have on your results. [3]
6. (a) Describe **one** alternative way of measuring your DV. [3]
   (b) Explain the effect this change may have on your results. [3]
7. (a) Describe **two** improvements that could have been made to your procedure. [3]
   (b) Explain the effects these improvements may have on the results of your activity. [3]
8. Identify an alternative design for your study. [1]
9. Explain the effects of implementing this alternative design in your study. [3]
10. (a) Describe **one** ethical issue you had to consider in your investigation. [2]
    (b) Explain how you overcame this ethical problem. [3]

PURPLE QUESTIONS: Examples of questions about self-report in general.

1. Outline **one** advantage of the experimental method. [2]
2. Outline **one** disadvantage of the experimental method. [2]
3. Outline **one** advantage of repeated measures design. [2]
4. Outline **one** disadvantage of repeated measures design. [2]
5. Outline **one** advantage of independent measures design. [2]
6. Outline **one** disadvantage of independent measures design. [2]
7. Outline **one** advantage of a field experiment. [2]
8. Outline **one** disadvantage of a field experiment [2]
9. Outline **one** advantage of laboratory experiments. [2]
10. Outline **one** disadvantage of laboratory experiments. [2]

Can you identify which questions on the facing page are green questions, blue questions and purple questions?

OCR Practical Activity C

Model answers to exam questions

Can you identify which questions are green questions, blue questions and purple questions?

1. Describe how your dependent variable was measured. [3]

The dependent variable was memory performance. This was measured by recalling a list of 20 words which had been previously presented to the participants. Words included television, museum, rug, donkey. They had up to a maximum of 3 minutes to recall the words, by writing them down on a sheet of paper. The sheet of paper was then taken away from each participant and the number of correct words counted up out of twenty and recorded.

2. (a) Describe an alternative way of measuring your dependent variable. [3]

As the DV is memory performance, this could be measured in another way. One way to measure this would be, instead of presenting a list of words and asking them to recall them, memory performance could be tested by recognition instead. This would involve giving participants a list of 40 words, twenty of which are the original words and the other twenty are distractor words which did not appear in the original list. Participants simply have to put a tick by the words which they recognize from the original list.

(b) Explain what effect this alternative would have on the results of the study. [3]

Recognising information is an easier task than recalling information because presenting them with words may remind them of the words, whereas doing it by recall they may just not be able to access the information in their mind as there are no clues. Therefore, I would expect that both groups of participants would get higher scores than measuring the DV in the original way. Having said that, recognition is still a valid measure of memory. But, I still think that there would be a difference between the two conditions (cued memory and non-cued memory) as there was such a difference in my investigation.

3. (a) Identify *one* ethical problem you had to consider when planning your investigation. [2]

One ethical issue is consent. We need to gain consent from participants to take part in an experiment. However, if we tell participants the aim of the study (to see if cued recall is better than non-cued recall) then participants may act differently due to demand characteristics.

3 (b) Explain how you overcame this ethical problem. [3]

We asked participants if they wanted to take part in a study of memory, but we did not tell them the true aim of the study (i.e. looking for differences between cued- and non-cued recall). This meant that although they knew they were going to be tested on their memory, that they could not guess which condition they were in, or which condition the other participants might be in. This meant that they would not be so prone to demand characteristics as this is using a kind of single-blind technique.

4. (a) Describe the sample that you used in your investigation. [3]

There were 20 participants, selected using an opportunity sampling technique as all were members of my A level class, 12 were female and 8 were male, all aged between 16 and 17 years old. Therefore, the parent population is A level students at my sixth form college in Cambridgeshire.

(b) Describe an alternative way of selecting a sample for your study. [3]

Another way would be to select the sample randomly, still using the same parent population (A level students at my sixth form college). I would get all the names of A level students in my college (there are about 900) and put them into a hat and then pick out twenty. I would then approach these twenty participants and ask them if they would take part in the study.

Examiner's comments

1. This is a very clear and detailed answer and would allow **replication** for anyone trying to measure a DV in the same way. Important details that this candidate has included are the number of words, the fact that they were written down (and not said out loud) and the time limit.

2. (a) This describes an appropriate and plausible alternative way of measuring the **DV**. This would receive full marks because it gives a very clear and detailed account of how this alternative could be achieved. This candidate may well have thought through an alternative **operationalisation** of the DV prior to the exam knowing that a question like this could come up.

2. (b) This is always quite a difficult and searching question. Again, advance preparation can pay off nicely. This is a particularly good answer because the candidate has dealt with both the raw results (increase in number of words overall) as well as the results of comparing the two conditions. Most importantly, the answer is clearly about the candidate's own **experiment**. Frequently, poorer answers make general comments about **validity** or **generalisability** without really relating it to their actual experiment.

3. (a) Again, this is a question that does not involve copying out of your folder but it is prudent to consider such questions before walking into the examination, just in case they pop up! The candidate here explains his quandary well. Importantly, this candidate has clearly related the **ethical** problem to their own study, rather than a more general answer about **consent**.

3. (b) Clear explanation of how the candidate resolved the ethical problem in an appropriate way, clearly related to the candidate's own investigation. The candidate's use of terminology (such as demand characteristics and single-blind technique) are used appropriately here.

4. (a) This merely involves copying out of the booklet. Usually, about a third or a half of the examination questions involve simply copying. This means you can get up to 50% of paper's marks just by making sure your booklet is filled in correctly in enough detail.

4. (b) This candidate has written about a **random sample** with definite understanding of what a random sample really is! Also, the candidate has related it well to how it could have been achieved in his own investigation.

OCR Practical Activity D

The practical investigations folder

On the left hand side of this spread you are shown how to fill in your folder for Activity D. The form produced by the board contains the titles (shown in black). Examiner's guidance is given for each title in green.

On the right hand side of this spread there is a *model* folder. You will use these answers for the green questions (see page 94) when you you sit your exam.

Guidance for filling in Practical Investigations Folder is given below.

Activity D: Collection of data involving two independent measures and analysis using a test of correlation.

State the hypothesis and null hypothesis for this activity.
Both hypotheses need to be stated very clearly. Each should include reference to the two variables which you are measuring. Make sure you predict a correlation between the two variables. For H_1, it is a good idea to state whether it is a one- or two-tailed hypothesis at the end in brackets.

Describe the two variables and how they were measured.
You can refer to each of these as Variable 1 and Variable 2. For each, you need to:
• Clearly state what the variable was (e.g. time spent traveling to college each day).
• Explicitly describe how it was measured.

Give details of the sample you used.
You should include:
• The type of sample used (probably opportunity sample).
• The number of participants.
• Age range of participants.
• Number of males and number of females.
• Where they were sourced from (e.g. your psychology class or your friends at college).
• Target (parent) population.

Summarise the procedure you used for this investigation.
A step-by-step version of your procedure so that it is replicable, including:
• Where your investigation was carried out.
• Time of day it was carried out.
• Details of instructions given to participants.
• Exact details of tasks participants had to undertake, including any time limits, description of materials etc.
• Details of any debrief administered.

Name the statistical test used to analyse your data
In all likelihood, this will be a Spearman's Rank Correlation Coefficient, as your data will be ordinal. See page 139 for how to calculate it.

Present your data using tables, visual displays and verbal summaries.
Ideally, you should include
• A small table of your data, with full title.
• A scattergraph of your data, with fully labelled axes and a title. A hand drawn scattergraph is fine and perhaps would allow you to copy it more readily in the examination if required rather than using a computer printout.
• A verbal description of your scattergraph – does the pattern suggest a positive or negative correlation between your two variables? Does it look like a weak or a strong correlation? Or is there no pattern discernible? These findings from your scattergraph do not provide information about significance! The scattergraph cannot tell us whether to accept or reject the null hypothesis. The Spearman's Rank Correlation Co-efficient is for that.

State the results of the statistical analysis.
State the value of Rho which you have calculated. Additionally, state the critical value of Rho for the appropriate number of participants, direction of your hypothesis and value of p. On this basis, you could say whether p is less than, or is greater than 0.05.

State your conclusions including statements of significance relating to the hypothesis.
Explain how, for the correlation to be significant, your calculated value of Rho must be bigger than the critical value of Rho. Describe whether your calculated Rho is smaller or bigger than the critical Rho, and corresponding value of p. Then you can say whether you should accept or reject your null hypothesis. Restate the hypothesis that you will accept.

You may attach a computer print out to this practical folder or record your calculations here.
This is optional. However, if you feel you are short of space in the box for presenting your data, this could be a way of including your raw data table.

Are sensation seeking and smoking related?

Activity D: Collection of data involving two independent measures and analysis using a test of correlation.

State the hypothesis and null hypothesis for this activity.

H_1 For smokers, there is a positive correlation between sensation seeking score on the SSS and the number of cigarettes smoked per day, as measured by self-report. (one-tailed)

H_0 For smokers, there is no correlation between sensation seeking score as measured by the SSS and the number of cigarettes smoked per day, as measured by self-report.

Describe the two variables and how they were measured.

IV1 – this is sensation seeking, as measured by a version of the Sensation Seeking Scale. This has 20 questions where the respondent has to choose between two alternative statements, (a) or (b). Maximum SS score = 20.

IV2 – this is the number of cigarettes per day the participant smokes as measured by self report in response to the question: "On average, how many cigarettes do you smoke per day?".

Give details of the sample you used.

This was an opportunity sample of 14 participants. All were smokers and were approached in the smoking area at my sixth form college in Cambridge. There were 8 males and 6 females, all aged between 16 and 18 years old. All were students at my sixth form college. Therefore the target population is students at my sixth form college in Cambridge who are smokers.

Summarise the procedure you used for this investigation.

In my free periods and break times in the week of 8 November, I approached participants in the smoking area at my sixth form college. I firstly asked them for consent to take part in a short study. If they consented, I asked them to fill in the sensation seeking questionnaire, which I gave to them, word processed, on a piece of paper, and gave them unlimited time to fill it in. When they had finished and handed back the questionnaire, I asked them : "On average, how many cigarettes do you smoke per day?", noting their response on the bottom of their questionnaire. I then thanked them for their time and debriefed them i.e. told them the aim of the research.

Name the statistical test used to analyse your data.

Spearman's Rho Rank Correlation Coefficient

Present your data using tables, visual displays and verbal summaries.

Participant	Sensation Seeking Score	No of Cigarettes Smoked per day
1	10	7
2	14	8
3	11	10
4	4	8
5	10	20
6	18	20
7	6	6
8	12	15
9	12	10
10	9	12
11	9	10
12	8	3
13	11	10
14	4	4

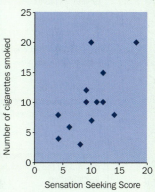

Scattergraph showing relationship between Sensation Seeking Score and No of Cigarettes Smoked per day

Looking at the scattergraph I can see that there is a noticeable, moderately positive correlation between the average number of cigarettes smoked and sensation seeking score.

State the results of the statistical analysis.

Calculated value of Rho = 0.603

Critical value Rho = 0.464 (n=14, p= 0.05, one tailed test)

Therefore, p<0.05 i.e. significant

State your conclusions including statements of significance relating to the hypothesis.

As the observed value of Rho (0.603) is greater than the critical value of Rho (0.464; n=14, p=0.05), this means that there is less than 5% doubt and more than 95% certainty that there is, for smokers, a positive correlation between average number of cigarettes smoked and sensation seeking score. So we can reject the null hypothesis and conclude that for smokers, there is a positive correlation between sensation seeking score on the SSS and the number of cigarettes smoked per day.

OCR Practical Activity D

The Blue Peter folder

Some of the questions in the exam involve copying from your PRACTICAL INVESTIGATIONS FOLDER; other questions involve more than just copying. It is more than a good idea to consider such possible questions before you are sitting at your little examination desk. Consider them now! A good idea is to create a BLUE PETER FOLDER (one that I prepared earlier) to write down all your ideas about improvements to each investigation, their effects upon results, key definitions and concepts etc. There is a blank version of the BLUE PETER FOLDER on the website (see www.nelsonthornes.com/researchmethods). This folder will get you ready for the blue questions (see page 94) so that you will have these answers 'up your sleeve' (so to speak) when you sit your exam.

*Suggest **one** problem with how you measured each of your variables.*	The problems will probably be different for each variable. Possible problems: • If you have used self-report for one variable, then possibly demand characteristics or social desirability bias may have lowered the validity of the data you have collected. • If you have used observation, then perhaps your **coding system** or rating scales caused problems. • Possibly some of the questions you have used were ambiguous or unclear. Remember to clearly relate your answer to your own investigation and explain why you perceive this to have been a problem.
Suggest an alternative way of measuring each of your variables.	Again, you may have to be quite inventive here. Think about what each of your variables is actually measuring e.g. memory or task performance or liking. If it is a memory test, you could switch a recall task for a recognition task, or vice versa. If you have measured task performance on a word search, you could switch it to task performance on a simple crossword, or series of mental arithmetic sums, and so on. There is always another way! Whatever you choose, make sure you describe it in detail!
Explain the effect each of these changes may have on your results.	Consider: • Whether it will change the significance level you found – more or less significant? • Whether your results will have more or less validity, generalisability, or ecological validity etc. • Will participants find this new task easier or more difficult?
*Describe **one** strength in the way that you conducted your investigation.*	Likely features to consider: • Good materials or tasks. • Any controls you used effectively. Explain why this feature of your investigation is a strength or what negative effects it prevented.
*Describe **one** weakness in the way that you conducted the procedure of your investigation.*	Whatever weakness you choose (there are probably several to choose from) then you should make it very specific to your own investigation. • A lack of control in some area: e.g. where you conducted your study may have been too noisy, or was not the same for each participant. • A possible weakness in the way you measured one of your variables: perhaps it lacked validity or ecological validity. • A problem with the materials you used. • Possibly the order in which you measured your variables caused some demand characteristics. Explain why this feature of your investigation is a weakness. What problems did it cause?
*Describe **one** improvement to the way that you conducted the procedure of your investigation.*	This could depend upon the weakness you identified above. But try to avoid an improvement to your sample. • A particular control which could be implemented. • A better way of measuring one of the two variables (see above). • A better (e.g. quieter) environment to conduct your correlation. Make sure you clearly contextualise your improvement in terms of your own activity.
Explain what effect this improvement may have on the results.	Consider: • Whether your results will show a stronger correlation (positive or negative) and are therefore more significant. • Whether your results will have more ecological validity, validity, generalisability etc.
*Describe **one** strength in the way that you selected your sample.*	Consider: • Size of sample – was it a large sample? • How representative is your sample of the target population i.e. who you wish to generalise to. • If you have a good range of ages or good mix of gender.
*Describe **one** weakness in the way that you selected your sample.*	Consider: • If you had a small sample. • If you only selected a very limited type of sample (e.g. one kind of student) and so it is not representative of your target population. • If it was heavily weighted towards one gender only. Remember to clearly relate your answer to your own investigation and your target population. Just saying 'lacks generalisability' would not receive much credit!
*Describe **one** improvement to the way that you selected your sample.*	Depends upon what you have identified above. Perhaps you could: • Use a random sample. • Use a stratified sample. • Gain a broader sample, or one more representative of your target population.
*Describe **one** ethical issue you had to consider in your investigation.*	Describe your improvement clearly and in detail, very clearly contextualised in terms of your own investigation. Your answer here will depend upon your investigation of course. Consider: • Consent – perhaps by gaining informed consent and telling participants about your study in advance you created some demand characteristics. • Harm or distress – perhaps if a participant performs badly in the task, it may lower their self-esteem.

Suggest one problem with how you measured each of your variables.

Variable 1: One problem with measuring sensation seeking with this questionnaire (developed by Zuckerman) was that participants had to choose between two sentences for each item. For example, on question 8, participants had to choose between "I like wild uninhibited parties" or "I prefer quiet parties with good conversation". This is really a forced choice and many participants said afterwards that they really wanted to answer along the lines of: "I like both but it depends on the situation" for many of the questions. Therefore, participants were often not able to give answers true to themselves, lowering the validity of measure.

Variable 2: (i.e. number of cigarettes smoked daily on average). This was measured by answering the question "On average, how many cigarettes do you smoke per day?" – this was a slightly vague question and did not necessarily get people to respond accurately or specifically. I got the feeling that some of the participants said 10 or 20 just because it was a nice round number and not because they had smoked exactly that many on average.

Suggest an alternative way of measuring each of your variables.

Variable 1: I could change the sensation seeking scale from choosing between two statements to a "semantic differential scale". This means that I would still have the two statements, but participants could choose a score one of 5 options:

Statement A	A	Tend to A	Both A and B	Tend to B	Statement B
I like wild, uninhibited parties					I prefer quiet parties with good conversation

This would allow participants to choose an option which most accurately reflects themselves.

Variable 2: Instead of asking people "On average, how many cigarette do you smoke per day?", I could do a kind of cigarette count. I could count the number of cigarettes they have in their packet at 9 am on one morning, and then count how many cigarettes they had at 9 am the following day. The difference would be how many cigarettes they had smoked in the preceding 24 hour period.

Explain the effect each of these changes may have on your results.

Variable 1: This would increase the validity of the sensation seeking scale. However, because it allows people to give more moderate answers (i.e. by using the middle option), then it could mean that many people give moderate answers reducing the range of scores. This may make my correlation less significant and I would not find a correlation between sensation seeking and smoking.

Variable 2: This would be more valid as people could not lie or forget or exaggerate etc. how many cigarettes they have on average. Therefore, the number is more trustworthy and valid. This may slightly vary the results but I don't think that overall it would affect the strength of the correlation as this new measure will increase some participant's scores slightly and decrease some participants' scores slightly, but not radically change the results.

Describe one strength in the way that you conducted your investigation.

One strength of this study was the order in which I measured the variables. Because I measured Sensation Seeking first (without participants really knowing what it was measuring) and then asked them about smoking, I think this meant that demand characteristics were reduced. Had I asked them about smoking first and then administered the SSS, then participants may have changed their

answers on the SSS to match how they wanted to be presented as a smoker. Therefore, SSS first and then asking about cigarettes helped to keep it a single blind technique.

Describe one weakness in the way that you conducted the procedure of your investigation.

One problem with my study was that it was conducted in the smoking area at my college. This is a small outdoor paved area. Mostly, it is quite busy. This meant that when a participant was filling in his/her questionnaire on sensation seeking, they may easily have become distracted by other people's conversations, or in some instances, by being asked for a light. This meant that some participants did not give their full concentration to the questionnaire.

Describe one improvement to the way that you conducted the procedure of your investigation.

I would improve this by approaching a participant in the smoking area (to ensure that I did actually approach a smoker) and then, once they had consented, take them to a quieter area e.g. an empty classroom at break time, or the library. This would mean the participant would be able to complete the questions with the minimum amount of distractions.

Explain what effect this improvement may have on the results.

This would improve the validity of the two variables as participants would be more able to answer the questions with more thought, rather than putting down an untrue response due to rushing or misreading a question. It might make the correlation between sensation seeking and number of cigarettes smoked stronger than in my investigation i.e. a more positive and significant correlation.

Describe one strength in the way that you selected your sample.

One strength in the way that I selected my sample was that it was an opportunity sample of people smoking in the smoking area at my college. This meant that I got a reasonable range of smokers – male and female – and not just smokers known to me personally through my classes. Consequently, they are quite representative of the target population i.e. smokers at my sixth form college in Cambridge.

Describe one weakness in the way that you selected your sample.

One weakness in the way that I selected my sample was that the sample was quite small. I estimate that there are about 100 students who smoke at my sixth form and I only collected data from 14 of them. This means that I may have, unwittingly, got a biased sample in some way that is not representative of smokers at my college. For example, I may have just got sensation-seeker smokers (who smoke to get a nicotine hit), rather than people who smoke in order to relieve stress.

Describe one improvement to the way that you selected your sample.

One improvement to my sample would be to gain a larger number of smokers and not just from my sixth form. I could do this by asking people at my place of work, family relations and friends and so on. This would create a larger and more diverse sample of smokers in terms of their ages, jobs and level of education. Therefore, I would be able to generalize my results to a broader target population.

Describe one ethical issue you had to consider in your investigation.

One ethical problem was that some of the items on the sensation seeking questionnaire were unethical, e.g. Item 10: the options were between (a) I would not like to try any drug which might produce strange and dangerous effects on me; and (b) I would like to try some of the drugs that produce hallucinations. Another item asked about use of stimulants and so on. I decided that such questions were too personal and possibly embarrassing. Therefore, I cut out those questions and only kept in items that would be inoffensive.

OCR Practical Activity D

Sample exam questions

See page 62 for an explanation of these questions.

Note that the questions provided here do not represent all the questions that may ever be asked but they do cover most of the possibilities.

These blue questions are the sort of questions which candidates find the most challenging. Practise the answers to these before the examination. Then you will be well prepared! You can do this by filling in the **BLUE PETER FOLDER**.

GREEN QUESTIONS: Examples of questions asking you to copy out of your practical investigation folder.

1. State the null hypothesis for your investigation. [3]

2. State the research hypothesis for your investigation. [3]

3. Explain how each of your variables was measured. [6]

4. Describe the sample you used for this activity. [3]

5. Describe the sampling method you used for this activity. [3]

6. Describe the procedure you followed when conducting your investigation. [4]

7. (a) Sketch an appropriately labelled visual display for your data. [3]

   (b) Outline one finding you can identify from this visual display. [3]

8. Name the statistical test you used to analyse the data. [3]

9. (a) State the results of your statistical analysis. [3]

   (b) Explain the conclusion that can be drawn from your statistical test. [3]

BLUE QUESTIONS: examples of questions about your activity but not involving copying from the folder.

1. (a) Suggest an alternative way of measuring **one** of your variables. [3]

   (b) Explain the effect this change may have on the results of your activity. [3]

2. Describe **one** strength of the sampling method you used in your investigation. [3]

3. Describe **one** weakness of the sampling method you used in your investigation. [3]

4. (a) Suggest an alternative sample you could have used in your investigation. [2]

   (b) Explain what effects this alternative sample may have had on the results of your investigation. [3]

5. (a) Describe **one** weakness in the way that you conducted your procedure. [3]

   (b) Describe **one** way of overcoming this weakness. [3]

   (c) Suggest an effect this improvement might have on the results of your activity. [3]

PURPLE QUESTIONS: Examples of questions about self-report in general.

1. Explain what is meant by a positive correlation. [3]

2. Explain what is meant by a negative correlation. [3]

3. Explain how you might use a correlation to test reliability. [3]

4. Explain how you might use a correlation to test validity. [3]

5. If a researcher finds that there is a positive correlation between people's stress level and the number of cups of coffee they consume, explain what you could conclude. [3]

Can you identify which questions on the facing page are green questions, blue questions and purple questions?

OCR Practical Activity D

Model answers to exam questions

1. (a) Explain how you measured the two variables in your investigation. [6]

IV1 – this is sensation seeking, as measured by a version of the Sensation Seeking Scale. This has 20 questions where the respondent has to choose between two alternative statements, (a) or (b). Sometimes (a) gets one point and sometimes (b) gets one point; e.g. question 8 a: "I like wild uninhibited parties" or b: "I prefer quiet parties with good conversation." Choice (a) here receives a point. Maximum SS score = 20.

IV2 –the number of cigarettes per day the participants smokes as measured by self report in response to the question: "On average, how many cigarettes do you smoke per day?".

(b) Describe *one* problem with how you measured one variable in your activity. [3]

IV2 – this was measured a bit vaguely as the question, "On average, how many cigarettes do you smoke a day?" did not necessarily get people to respond accurately or specifically. I got the feeling that some of the participants said 10 or 20 just because it was a nice round number & not because they had smoked exactly that many on average.

(c) Suggest an improvement in the way that you measured this variable. 3]

Instead of asking "On average, how many cigarettes do you smoke per day?", I should have asked each participant: "How many cigarettes exactly did you smoke yesterday?". This seems to be cueing a more specific and therefore accurate response.

(d) Explain how this change to the measurement of a variable might affect the results of your activity. [3]

I think I may end up with a similar level of correlation overall. This is because it will stop a number of people from just saying 10 or 20 – which may strengthen the correlation. However, yesterday's number of cigarettes smoked may not be a typical or representative day. It might have been a particularly stressful day; or they had run out etc. Therefore, it may not show the true relationship to a person's level of sensation seeking. All in all, it will give a similar level of positive correlation between smoking and sensation seeking.

2. (a) Sketch an appropriately labelled visual display for your data. [3]

Scattergraph showing relationship between sensation Seeking and No. Cigarettes Smoked per day

(Scattergraph: y-axis "Number of cigarettes smoked" marked 5, 10, 15, 20, 25; x-axis "Sensation seeking score" marked 0, 5, 10, 15, 20)

(b) Outline *one* conclusion from this visual display. [3]

As the observed value of Rho (0.603) is greater than the critical value of Rho (0.464; n=14, p=0.05), this means that there is less than 5% doubt and more than 95% certainty that there is, for smokers, a positive correlation between average number of cigarettes smoked and sensation seeking score. So we can reject the null hypothesis.

3. (a) Describe what is meant by a negative correlation. [3]

This means that as one variable decreases, the other variable also decreases. In other words, both variables are indirectly proportional.

(b) A researcher looking at students' lifestyles, discovers that there is a negative correlation between number of fruit and vegetable portions eaten per day, and number of days off college. What could you conclude from these findings? [3]

I could conclude that amount of fruit and vegetables eaten affects how many days off a student has. This is probably because people who eat lots of fruit and veg are healthier and so do not need days off. But people who do not each much fruit and vegetables are a lot less healthy and so get ill more easily, therefore having lots more days off.

Examiner's comments

1. (a) This is a good, full answer. The examiner would not have any question about how either of the variables were measured – so full marks!

1. (b) Good answer – very specific to the candidate's activity and not superficial. Of course, the few self-reports of 10s and 20s in the data could be because cigarettes come in that size packet and so that is a person's 'ration' for a day. But it is still a plausible answer.

1. (c) This may be a relatively short answer, but there is enough here for 3 marks. The candidate has addressed the problem identified in part (b) and given some rationale for why this would work.

1. (d) As a candidate, you can appreciate the importance of being acquainted with the 'blue questions' before the exam, so that you do not come unstuck later on. This candidate has probably considered such a series of questions before the exam, as their answer here is quite a thoughtful response and really deals with the effect upon the results.

2. (a) 'Visual display' always means graph or chart, rather than raw data table. The candidate has copied this scattergraph out of their booklet correctly. Both axes are labelled fully with an appropriate title. Generally, for each missing label, a mark would have been deducted.

2. (b) Uh-oh! This candidate has misread the question and gone down the wrong track, talking about the conclusion from the statistical test, and not from the scattergraph. This would get 0/3. This is because scattergraphs do not tell us anything at all about the significance of the results, or whether the null hypothesis can be accepted or not.

3. (a) Uh-oh! This candidate is beginning to go to pieces… this is a fairly typical error, the candidate 'reverses' the definition learnt for positive correlation, but becomes unstuck. The second sentence is, however, correct. Thus 1/ 3.

3. (b)This is a trap! Look before you leap! Think before you write! Remember, that, however tempting it looks, however common sensical it may seem, that correlations NEVER tell us about cause and effect. All that this correlation tells us is that the two variables are inversely related. In other words, the more fruit and vegetables consumed, the fewer days' absence; and vice versa. So, this answer would receive 0 marks.

*Look before you leap!
Think before you write!*

Coursework

There are two written pieces of coursework you need to produce:

1. The Practical Project;

2. The Assignment.

The **Practical Project** involves you conducting your own piece of research, not dissimilar from your AS practical investigations. The main difference is that you will have to write a report of the research using a standard report format and refer to background research.

The **Assignment** involves you using your knowledge about psychology to explain events recounted in a recent newspaper article. You will write this up in a kind of essay format.

There are three guiding principles in producing your coursework:

1. Keep to the word limit.

   • For the Practical Project this is 1400 words.

   • The assignment limit is just 1000 words.

   This means you will have to use a very concise style of writing.

2. Simple projects/assignments are more likely to get full marks. This is because simple projects/assignments produce simple data which can be easily analysed and discussed within the word limit.

3. You want to get full marks. The coursework (project + assignment) is worth 16.6% of your final A level mark. This is potentially a gift from the exam board because you can get nearly all the marks if you listen to advice.

Contents

COURSEWORK

PRACTICAL PROJECT 1: SEX STEREOTYPES

Grade A project: The method

Page 4 of the report

Methodology

Design and Sample
This was a content analysis of UK TV advertisements on 5 weekday evenings between 7.00 p.m. and 10.00 p.m. using the ITV channel. One variable (or category) was whether the product authority (i.e. the person presenting the product) was male or female and the other variable was whether this was a voice-over or visual product authority. In another sense, it could be considered to be a natural experiment as the main IV is comparing such results collected in 2004, with those results collected in 1981 by Manstead and McCulloch to see if gender-role stereotyping has moved on since then.

Materials
TV, videotape and video recorder, table/chart to record findings.

The chart/table form and contents was designed by Manstead and McCulloch(1981) and sets out specific criteria to categorise and assess sex stereotyping of males and females in TV advertising (see appendix). 96 advertisements were recorded over a five-day period. Videotaping allowed more time and a greater degree of accuracy in relating adverts to specified criteria. (See Results section for Table.)

Page 5 of the report

Procedure

I set the video to record 3 hours of TV on the ITV channel each evening from Monday to Friday evenings between 7.00 p.m. and 10.00 p.m. for one week in April 2004. The data were collected and analysed at the end of the week so that duplicated adverts could be discarded. This would have been more difficult to do if data had been collected at the end of each evening or complicated the process by actual adverts having to be recorded to avoid duplication. It would also have made the study less valid if the duplicated advertisement had been included. The timing of recording was chosen to mirror Manstead and McCulloch's procedure but was a little less than their 6.30 p.m. to 11.00 p.m. time period. They chose Granada TV and I selected ITV as this is a comparable station.

Using the Table each advert was analysed and the criteria selected e.g. male or female voice-over or visual (depending on which was the stronger 'authority' figure), location/setting of advert, autonomous or dependent role of main figure etc.

Some other advertisements were also discarded where there was total emphasis on the product with no voice-over or specific figure and cartoon adverts where sex was indeterminate.

As this material is already in the public domain the ethics of the study can be rated as very good.

Methodology	**Band 3:** There is a clear rationale for the aim/hypotheses	**Actual marks: 7 out of 8.**

Methodology (*4 marks*)
Marks are awarded for:

The main criteria for awarding marks in this section is whether you have provided sufficient detail for your study to be replicated (repeated) by someone else.

The method is like writing a recipe for a cake. You need to provide every detail so that someone else could do the same thing → replication.

It is not just a matter of whether someone could conduct a *similar* study but whether they could do the *exact* same study. If someone varies small details, such as kind of participants, this may explain why the findings differ, so replication must be identical as far as possible in order to validate the original findings

→ 3-400 words is about right for the method section.

Useful subheadings to use include: design and sample (including sampling procedure), materials (actual examples to be placed in the appendix and described/referenced here), and procedure (including, for example, how participants were allocated to conditions and referenced to the appendix).

Things to put in the appendix (as appropriate): standardised instructions (briefing and debriefing), examples of materials, maps, etc.

By evaluating here, there is a little loss of conciseness. This explains why the candidate has not quite achieved full marks.

This is a slightly unusual study as it is a content analysis. This procedure is replicable and a stranger to this study would have no problem in copying it.

This is about 300 words, a short 'methodology' section because the study is very straightforward. There is sufficient detail for full replication.

Grade A project: The results

Page 6 of the report

Results

Table One

Comparison of Male and Female authority figures in 1981 and 2004 in TV commercials. *(1981 figures from Manstead and McCulloch).*

Authority Figures	1981	2004
Male (Voice-overs)	67%	63%
Female (Voice-overs)	7%	44%
Male (Visual)	32%	36%
Female (Visual)	92%	56%

Please see appendices for Manstead and McCulloch original data.

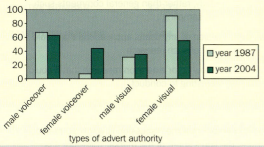

Bar chart showing percentages of males and female as product authorities, either visual or voiceover

Legend: year 1987, year 2004

types of advert authority

x-axis labels: male voiceover, female voiceover, male visual, female visual

---

Page 7 of the report

The table shows that the percentages for male authority figures have changed very little since 1981 – a slight increase in the visual and decrease in the voice-over. However, the percentages for female authority figures has changed significantly. Whereas in 1981 95% of the visual roles were female, this has dropped to 56% in 2004. The reverse is true of voiceovers where there has been a significant increase in female voiceovers changing from only 7% in 1981 to 44% in 2004.

There is still a large discrepancy of 20% more male authority figures in voice-overs than females and interestingly 20% less males in the visual role.

Performing a chi-square Test on this data, I found that chi -square = 35.97.

Critical value chi-square = 16.27 (df = 3, p=0.001 two-tailed)

Because the calculated value of chi-square is greater than the critical value, p <0.001 I can reject the null hypothesis and accept the research hypothesis, that there has been a significant change in sex role stereotyping in the last 23 years.

Results	**Band 3:** The appropriate use of summaries, tables, visual displays and an inferential test clearly and concisely describes and demonstrates an understanding of the data, their analyses and conclusions.	**Actual marks: 8 out of 8.**

Results *(8 marks)* Marks are awarded for:

Summary table of data, some kind of visual display e.g. bar chart/pie chart, a verbal description of the data, results of a statistical analysis and the corresponding conclusion.

Summary table of data.

This may well be a table of measures of central tendency and dispersion as appropriate (e.g. mean, median, mode, and/or range).

For this study measures of central tendency/dispersion are not appropriate as the data are nominal (categorical). A more appropriate table would be a frequency table or table of percentages, as shown here.

A visual display should be included.

This could be a bar chart of mean values, or a frequency polygon, or a pie chart. You only need to provide *one* of these. For a correlation, you should plot a scattergraph! Make sure you label the axes and give it a full title.

Do not just plot participants along the x-axis and scores on the y-axis! This does not help show any pattern or difference in the data.

This verbal description of the data helps the reader pick out the most important information from the data. It is written well and shows good understanding.

Unless you have collected purely qualitative data, you should do an inferential statistical test, state your results and your conclusions.

If the data are qualitative then you need to analyse themes in your data, providing a thorough written summary and analysis.

N.B. You are more likely to get more marks for quantitative data.

This phrase shows understanding of why the candidate has accepted the research hypothesis and rejected the null hypothesis.

PRACTICAL PROJECT 2: ATTRIBUTION OF RESPONSIBILITY

Grade C project: The introduction, method and results

Page 2 of the report

Hypotheses

H_1: Participants told the story with the more serious consequences give a higher rating of stupidity (on a scale of 1 to 10) than participants told the story with the less serious consequences (one tailed).

H_0: There is no difference in the rating of stupidity (on a scale of 1 to 10) for the participants told the story with the serious consequences compared to the participants told the story with the less serious consequences.

Hypotheses	**Band 2:** There is a clear research aim and, as appropriate, clearly operationalised experimental / correlational and null hypotheses.	**Actual marks: 3 out of 3**

Methodology

Design: An independent measures design i.e. the experimental and control groups consist of different participants, who only perform in one condition of the IV. The independent variable being the consequences of the story told to participants (serious versus minor consequences) and the dependent variable being the strength of attribution as measured by rating of the stupidity of the driver on a scale of one to ten.

Sample: An opportunity sample. Participants were 20 people, 10 males and 10 females all known to me, friends, family and work colleagues aged between 20 and 55 years. I randomly allocated them to the conditions.

Procedure: 20 people were asked for their consent to take part in answering the following question;
A man parks his car at the top of the hill, he forgets to put the handbrake on and the car rolls down the hill and ….
A) hits a tree (less serious consequences)
B) hits a shop window injuring a shopkeeper and a small child (serious consequences)

10 participants were told part A of the story and were asked to rate the 'stupidity' of the driver for forgetting to put on his handbrake on a scale of one to ten. The other 10 participants were told part B of the story and asked to rate the 'stupidity' of the driver on a scale of one to ten (ten being the most stupid). All participants were debriefed.

Methodology Overall, replication is generally possible, but there are a few details missing/unclear, such as how exactly participants were randomly allocated to the two conditions; or the means by which participants responded to 'the question' – on paper or verbally etc.

Methodology	**Band 2:** The methodology is described, with some minor omissions, but replication is possible.	**Actual marks: 5 out of 8**

Page 3 of the report

Controls: Standardised instructions – see appendix.

Materials: Both part A and B of the story were typed out on separate pieces of paper and given to each participant. Standardised instructions – see appendix.

Results

Table of results showing scores of stupidity for the serious consequences and less serious consequences

	A (not serious consequences)	B (serious consequences)
Mean	6.2	8.6
Median	7	9
Mode	7	10
Range	7	5

Statistical test: The statistical test used for this data is the Mann-Whitney U test (as the data was ordinal, independent measures design, looking for a difference between two conditions).

The calculated (observed) value of U = 16. Critical value of U = 16 (n = 10, 10, p = 0.005)

Because the calculated value of U (16) is the same as the critical value of 16. p = 0.005 and therefore we can reject the null hypothesis and accept the experimental hypothesis that participants told the story with the more serious consequences give a higher rating of stupidity than the participants told the story with the less serious consequences.

Ideally, this **results** section should have included a visual display, such as a bar chart of the means and a brief discussion of the chart and table, in order to demonstrate a clear understanding of the results; however, the discussion of the inferential test (Mann-Whitney) is clear and appropriate.

Results	**Band 2:** The data are recorded and analysed in a comprehensible form, with appropriate use of the following: summaries, tables, visual displays, an inferential test; the key aspects of the findings are presented clearly.	**Actual marks: 5 out of 8**

Page 4 of the report

Discussion:

I found there was a significant difference between the two conditions. The story with the serious consequences has overall been given a higher rating of stupidity by participants because of the damage caused when the car hit the shop window, injuring the shopkeeper and a small child. The story with the less serious consequences only hit a tree therefore not causing as much damage. This relates to the study by Walster who also found that participants would blame the driver of the car if the consequences were more serious. This shows that people do not judge people by their actions, but by the consequences of their actions.

Methodological problems encountered were the wording of the question. Participants were asked to rate how stupid the driver was for forgetting to put his handbrake on. Some participants said he was not stupid but that he was forgetful; i.e. participants were making a different attribution to the one I was offering. I could improve a future replication by using different wording, i.e. asking participants to rate the 'responsibility' of the actor. This would be more similar to Walster's original procedure.

My sample was reasonable in that there was a broad age range. But it could have been improved by having a larger sample.

Ethically, the study was quite sound as participants gave consent, could withdraw and were debriefed. However, perhaps the scenario may have caused some distress if they had been involved in a car crash.

One good thing about an independent measures design is you do not get demand characteristics, as participants only saw one scenario and only answered one question. The drawback with using an independent measures design in this study is that a participant may have had a past experience with a car accident therefore giving a higher rating and affecting the results. However, it may be possible to screen out participants who have been involved in car accidents and this would ensure a more even matching of participant variables across the two groups.

Page 5 of the report

Another problem with this study is that the scenario was very brief and only included the information the researcher thought important. This is unlike a real life scenario where many other details would also have been present, impacting on the observers' attributions. A future study could try to improve the ecological validity by having a video. However, this would be difficult to find or manufacture.

For further research in this area, it would be interesting to look at real life case studies to see whether the sentences handed out are based on the consequences of the action (even if unintended) rather than the action itself.

References

Walster 1966 in:
Gross, R.D. (1992) *Psychology: Science of Mind and Behaviour* (2ⁿᵈ edition). London: Hodder and Stoughton.
Appendices included

NB appendices not included in this text, but consisted of standardized instructions, materials, raw data collected, workings for statistical test.

Grade C project: The discussion

First impression: this **discussion** looks too short, considering that it is worth 25% of the marks.

While it is often a good idea to begin the discussion by relating your findings to the background research/context, this seems a little thin and superficial, and does not really move on from the results section.

The final sentence in this paragraph shows a good understanding of the conclusion of this study.

Some methodological weaknesses addressed here, with some discussion of improvements.

This is a bit weak (and sadly all too common a comment). It does not explain why a larger sample is always better. Also it does not really engage with the candidate's study; it could almost apply to any study. Remember that it is really important to make all your comments truly engage with the research that you conducted.

Ethics mentioned here.

This discussion has hit many issues, but does not always show a thorough understanding of the research process or that the candidate has really reflected upon their own research. Thus, while it does not completely constitute a 'list-like' approach to discussion, it is not worthy of top band marks and would receive top of band 2.

Discussion	**Band 2:** The project is evaluated, demonstrating some understanding of the research process. Evaluative points are made which, where appropriate, may refer to the psychological context, the methodology, ethical considerations, and suggestions for improvements or future research. They may be list-like or simply observations.	**Actual marks: 6 out of 10**
Presentation and Communication	**Band 2:** The report, its references and appropriate appendices are presented clearly and concisely, in the standard format.	**Actual marks: 4 out of 4**

TOTAL MARK
27/40

The total represents a safe grade C.

THE ASSIGNMENT

Based on an article from "The Guardian" Newspaper January 2004

A life cut short by prejudice

Part A

My first assumption is intergroup discrimination. The article reports that "they called her a freak….Tranny Paula", shouted abuse and "daubed graffiti on the walls of her flat". Paula did not belong to a 'socially acceptable' group in the Lancashire village because she was born male but dressed female. Tajfel's intergroup discrimination experiments (1970) were set in a more benign environment clearly demonstrating outgroup discrimination even in randomly allocated groupings. Because Paula is perceived as belonging to another group, she suffers out-group discrimination.

My second assumption is gender identity. Sexual identity is determined by biological factors but gender identity is a person's own awareness of being male or female. Paula was born biologically male but by the age of 14 had a strong desire to be female. Even before that her mother noted that Paula "was quite an unusual child….she grew her hair and looked a lot more feminine….I wondered if she was gay". The mother of a girl friend of Paul(a) phoned to say "he was very depressed……he said he wanted to be a girl". Money and Erhardt (1972) based their study primarily on hermaphrodites, demonstrating that "physical characteristics of sex seem to be … unimportant in terms of the ultimate gender role characteristic that the individual eventually adopts".

My third assumption is the internalisation of bullying. "It was humiliating when we were out . People … shouting abuse at her…. I don't know how she put up with it for 10 years". Paula internalised this bullying like some of the prisoners in Zimbardo's study (1973), became depressed, anxious and upset. A schoolfriend's mother reported that "he was very depressed …… worried he would do something to himself". Similarly, Zimbardo's participants showed signs of extreme despair as a results of the bullying.

Page 2 of the assignment

Part B

In intergroup discrimination theory Tajfel demonstrates that merely being categorised creates intergroup discrimination behaviour. Tajfel randomly allocated boys to two groups (e.g. over and underestimators) asking them to allocate points. Tajfel found the perception of someone belonging to another group caused ingroup favouritism and outgroup discrimination. Paula is perceived to belong to an outgroup by the residents in her small Lancashire village. As a result of this, they showed extreme forms of discrimination towards her ranging from name calling, physical bullying and damage to property. Only in Brighton, a famously perceived liberal and more tolerant environment, where she lived with a boyfriend did she feel accepted.

Money and Erhardt's (1972) findings show that a number of individuals are unhappy with the physical sex into which they were born. If such discontentment persists they may decide to undertake a gruelling process which eventually results in changing or reassigning their sex. Their study states that "most transsexuals report that they have felt very strong feelings of being born into the wrong type of body from quite an early age". Paula "realised (s)he wanted to be a girl when (s)he was 14 years old". Her mother says "she grew her hair and she looked a lot more feminine. She would pull her jeans in to show off her waist". A psychiatrist diagnosed her as transsexual after an hour's consultation and sent her to London to a specialist in "'gender problems". He explained that "all foetuses start as female and then there are changes in the brain which make it male". Money and Erhardt note that "changing sex is an arduous process….one which frequently involves social rejection from friends, family or employers".

This assignment is based on a newspaper article about a 24-year-old transsexual, who started life as male but chose to become female. (S)he endured years of abuse at school and in her home village, eventually, it seems, throwing herself fatally under a car. To see the full article, visit http://www.guardian.co.uk/Archive/ and tap in the title.

This assignment clearly and swiftly identifies the three assumptions, one in each paragraph.

The word limit for the newspaper assignment is very tight. This assignment tries to keep within the word limit by editing quotes down to the absolutely essential bits!

In each paragraph, the psychology is briefly outlined in a couple of sentences, keeping focused on the most relevant bits of the research. This helps to develop a strong argument.

These paragraphs make more than just a link between the psychology and the source: they explain, in just enough detail, *why* each bit of psychology relates to events covered in the article, or draw appropriate parallels between the source and the study.

Issues/Assumptions	**Band 3: 7-9 marks:** A range of appropriate psychological issues / assumptions, from at least two different areas of psychology and raised by the source, is clearly and concisely identified, justified and related to appropriate psychology.	**Actual marks: 9 out of a maximum of 9**

The second section of this assignment is again well structured, taking a paragraph for each of the three assumptions. This structure will help endear you to the examiner, as well as aiding him or her in reading your work.

This paragraph describes the relevant evidence in the first few sentences …

and then carefully uses the psychology to explain the events in the source. In some cases, several parallels between the evidence and the source are established. This goes further than Part A (a) in terms of its detail and depth of explanation.

Page 3 of the Assignment

Zimbardo's 1973 Stanford University mock prison experiment showed that as the guards became more aggressive, dominant and bullying in their behaviour towards the prisoners, the latter became more frustrated and either conformed or internalised the bullying resulting in Pathological Prisoner Syndrome: "extreme depression … uncontrollable crying and fits of rage". These prisoners had internalised the lack of power and continual ridicule, resulting in a negative self-image. Paula did nothing to incite the bullying apart from being a transsexual. Similarly, Zimbardo's prisoners were often subjected to bullying for no other reasons than they were prisoners and easy targets. Their depression, anxiety and illness resulted in the experiment being stopped after 6 days. Paula experienced extreme and prolonged bullying for considerably longer than Zimbardo's 6 days. In many ways, it is surprising Paula did not kill herself much earlier.

Part C

Intergroup discrimination theory is found on many levels in a multitude of life environments. School years often foster groupings including race, sporting or academic ability, preference of football team, social class and gender. Tajfel's experiments were set in a Bristol school with pupils seemingly selected but actually randomly allocated to groups. Taking these theories and their consequences into the school environment could act as life learning skills via role play, drama, RE etc. An enforcing agent would be real life experiences from those in and outside the school environment. Paula could have benefited from greater tolerance from an earlier age. If schoolfriends had greater awareness this may have helped protect her from the ignorance of the wider environment. It is easy for a single person to be a target. However, backup from the home environment, or lack of it, can negate the endeavours of the educators.

Page 4 of the Assignment

Transsexuals/vestites are often perceived as choosing to do/be so but this is not usually the case. Using role models such as Eddie Izzard (as suggested by Bandura's Social Learning Theory) and others more accepted and well known in the media can be useful to educate and doing so via schools using English, Drama and, particularly facts in Biology, would increase knowledge and understanding. The biggest influence will be the passage of time – or maybe David Beckham becoming a woman!

Internalisation of bullying is hard to turnaround. Paula was bullied from an early age but a system of mentoring or 'buddying' with students of older years taking responsibility for younger students could be successful. A zero tolerance approach (developed out of behaviourist principles) by a school reinforces the non-acceptance but will not necessarily mean that those being bullied will reveal the problem. This could also be adopted by the working environment as adulthood does not necessarily mean no bullying. Despite the school age problem, if Paula had managed to have a job/career with a mentor, the signals of acceptance would have been clearer and may have perpetrated to the social environment. However, time may again play an important role in future acceptance and understanding.

References

Tajfel 1970; Haney Banks and Zimbardo 1968; Bandura 1961 cited in
Gross, R.D., 3rd edition "Key Studies in Psychology", 1999, London, Hodder and Stoughton.
Money and Erhardt (1972) cited in
Gross, R.D. 2nd edition "Psychology: Science of Mind and Human Behaviour" 1996, London, Hodder and Stoughton.

The evidence that is described is appropriately detailed. Although some of your assumptions may be based on very familiar core studies, it is important, even in this section, to limit yourself to the facts of the study that are most relevant to the article. For example, with the Zimbardo prison study, rather than write about all the details of the participants, induction procedure, the guard's behaviour etc. this candidate has cleverly concentrated on the bits of the study most relevant i.e. the effect of bullying and how this becomes internalized.

Evidence	**Band 4: 12-15 marks:** Apposite and detailed psychological evidence is presented clearly, concisely and accurately, and is explicitly related to the source. The evidence demonstrates an understanding of different areas of psychology.	**Actual marks: 13 out of max 15**

Each paragraph is carefully structured to hit all targets on the markscheme:

The psychology bit.

The suggestion…

…linked to the source (i.e. how it may have affected Paula).

Evaluation of the suggestion.

The candidate has done everything in this paragraph except link it to the source; thus this section cannot get absolutely full marks.

The second and third suggestions refer to different psychology from that presented in the earlier parts, but to great effect!

What this section also demonstrates is a particularly fine understanding of both the suggestion and the psychology upon which it is based. This is one of the things that pushes this section into Band 3, rather than Band 2; i.e. it has 'pragmatic and perceptive understanding'.

Applications	**Band 3: 8-10 marks:** The suggestions apply apposite psychological knowledge explicitly to the issues/assumptions raised in the source, from different areas of psychology. They are based on apposite psychological evidence, related explicitly to the source, showing perceptive and pragmatic understanding and evaluation.	**Actual marks: 9 out of a max of 10**

Overall, this assignment is within the word limit (992 words). The candidate clearly understands and uses a range of psychological terms. All the references are noted in the standard format.

Presentation & communication	**Band 3: 5-6 marks:** The assignment is concise and coherent displaying a good understanding of a wide range of psychological terms. All references are noted in the text and supplied in the standard format.	**Actual marks: 6 out of a max of 6**

TOTAL MARKS 37/40

Grade C assignment

THE ASSIGNMENT

Baghdad Blogger goes to Washington: Day 2

(a)

My first assumption is that our assessment or perception of people is based mainly upon the situation in which we see them. This is seen in the article where Salam Pax ("the Baghdad Blogger") meets up with an American soldier, Sean, while in Washington DC. "When I told him I would never actually approach an American soldier on the street in Baghdad, he told me that if we were in Baghdad he would probably be talking to me with his gun pointing at me because he would be scared shitless. Yet there [in Washington] we sat, drinking beers together." This relates to Rosenhan's initial hypothesis in his article "Being Sane in Insane Places" as he asserts that we judge people according to the situation in which we see people. Had Sean seen Pax on a Baghdad street, he would have perceived him as a potential threat; yet on safe ground, they are sitting there, getting to know each other over beer, treating each other as individuals.

My second assumption is classical conditioning i.e. learning through association. Both Pax and Sean have learnt to associate loud bangs with gunfire, leading to fear reactions. "We exchange stories about how badly both of us are dealing with sounds of things popping. He tells me he will never again go to a July 4 celebration because of the fireworks, and I tell him how I got laughed at when I ducked and ran after a car backfired near me in London. " This links to Pavlov's research on dogs, who found that they could link a neutral stimulus (bell) with another stimulus (food) to produce the same reaction, salivation.

This assignment is based upon an article written by the 'Baghdad blogger' (Salam Pax) published in October 2004. In the run-up to war, Pax published a diary on the web from his home in Baghdad, describing the days before the beginning of the war. This article was written after the official end of hostilities when Pax visited the US. It is an interesting individual take on the effects of the war. The original article can be viewed on http://www.guardian.co.uk/Iraq/Story/0,276,1332786,00.htm

Please note, that the standard, even of a grade C assignment, is still quite good!

This first assumption paragraph lacks the necessary conciseness.

This assignment clearly introduces each of the three assumptions, linking them to evidence and providing an explanation of their relevance. However, not all assumptions are concisely explained.

Page 2 of the assignment

My third assumption is that Sean, as a serving soldier, experiences a non-agentic state. Talking of going to fight in Iraq, he says: "I was there because I was ordered to be there. That is my reason, my sole reason. My personal feelings mean nothing. I was not asked and I will not be asked. I'm cool with that .. because I don't work in a democracy - I work for one." Like the Milgram obedience study, where participants went against their natural conscience to obey an authority figure, Sean too has put aside his own personal views when serving in the army.

(b)

The evidence for my first assumption is Rosenhan. In his article, "Being Sane in Insane Places", at the outset he states that we judge people according to the situation that we meet them in. In this study, one of Rosenhan's aims was to find out whether a person, behaving normally in a mental hospital, is perceived as normal, or whether the situation holds more sway over attributions and because someone is in a mental hospital it makes people perceive them as mentally ill. This is what Rosenhan found. For example, one of the pseudo patients was accused of having "oral acquisitive syndrome" just for waiting for the cafeteria to open. Similarly in the article, it shows that the situation in which we meet a person is more powerful than reading any cues directly from that person, as Sean says that were he to encounter Pax in Baghdad, he would have been pointing his gun at him in expectation of the attack.

The evidence for my second assumption is Pavlov. Pavlov found that dogs can learn by association. He accidentally found that the laboratory dogs would salivate to the sound of a bell, and decided to investigate this further. He repeatedly paired up meal times (unconditioned stimulus) with a bell (conditioned stimulus) and found that soon, the bell would produce the same response, salivation (conditioned response). This is classical conditioning. Pax and Sean both, from the experiences during the war in Iraq, now associate loud popping noises (conditioned stimulus) with gunfire. Now, just popping noises produce the same reaction, i.e. fear. Sean says he cannot cope with the fireworks at a July 4th event and Pax tells of diving for cover when a car backfired in London.

Issues/Assumptions	**Band 3: 7-9 marks:** A range of appropriate psychological issues / assumptions, from at least two different areas of psychology and raised by the source, is clearly and concisely identified, justified and related to appropriate psychology.	**Actual mark: 7 out of a maximum of 9**

The evidence from Rosenhan is nicely focused on the aspects of the study which are most relevant to this assumption, and the candidate at this point has not fallen into the trap of wasting words on details of the study which are not relevant!

The use of the evidence to explain Sean's comments in the article demonstrates good understanding.

The description of Pavlov's classic piece of research is not very concise, but does demonstrate reasonable understanding.

"I DON'T KNOW ABOUT YOU, BUT THAT BELL'S STARTING TO PUT ME OFF MY FOOD!"

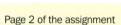

Page 3 of the assignment

The evidence for my third assumption comes from Milgram's 1963 experiments on obedience. Milgram was interested in why Nazi death camp guards followed orders and committed such atrocious acts. He conducted an experiment on ordinary Americans. When they arrived at the laboratory, they were met by the experimenter and introduced to another man who was apparently another participant, but who was a stooge. They were told they would be taking part in a study of learning. The stooge became the learner and the participant took the role of teacher. The teacher was instructed by the experimenter to administer shocks to the learner, but in fact these shocks were fake. Surprisingly, 65% of participants gave the highest possible shock level (450 volts), even though it was clearly going against their own conscience and wish not to seriously harm another human. This is like the source as Sean says that his personal beliefs about fighting in Iraq do not matter as he was ordered to be there, and he just followed orders. He abdicates his responsibility to "the democracy that [he] works for", that is the American government.

(c)
My suggestion for the first assumption is that soldiers should be trained in how to deal with civilians whilst in enemy territory so that they can more objectively assess whether they are a threat or just an ordinary civilian. This would mean that they would be able to treat civilians more normally, without constant suspicion and physically pointing guns at every innocent passer-by. This could mean that the American soldiers in Iraq would gain more support from everyday Iraqi's. However, one problem with this is that in doing so, soldiers may put themselves at more risk from suicide bombers and ambushes.

Page 4 of the assignment

My suggestion for the second assumption is that Pax and Sean undergo some behaviourist therapy known as "extinction"; this is where someone experiences the conditioned stimulus many times without it being associated with the original unconditioned stimulus. Thus, Pax and Sean would have to be exposed to lots of loud popping noise, in a safe environment with no gunfire or threat. Eventually, they would learn to disassociate popping noises from gunfire and be able to react more normally, without fear reactions.

My suggestion for the third assumption is that it becomes easier for soldiers to become "conscientious objectors" i.e. be able to opt out of fighting in certain wars if they do not believe there is adequate mandate or reason to go to war. However, this could mean that many soldiers refuse to fight, leaving a country in a vulnerable situation. Also, some soldiers may use it as an excuse!

References
Gross, R.D., 3rd edition "Key Studies in Psychology", 1999, London, Hodder and Stoughton.

The use of this piece of evidence is probably the weakest. The candidate fails to focus on the most salient parts of the study. It would have been better had they given fewer details of the actual study and then perhaps progressed to Milgram's ideas of agentic and non-agentic states (as mentioned in part a), as this provides a really strong explanation of Sean's comments in the article.

This paragraph will slightly bring down the marks as it lacks some of the top, band 4, requirements, such as conciseness because there is too much irrelevant detail.

Evidence	Band 3: Apposite psychological evidence is described clearly and concisely and with understanding. It is explicitly related to the source.	Actual marks: 10 out of a maximum 15

This third section is often the most problematic, and certainly it is the weakest of the three sections in this assignment. Many of the suggestions lack some of the vital elements.

No link to evidence; but it does have a decent suggestion, linked directly to the source, and there is an evaluation of the suggestion.

This suggestion needs some more explicit evaluation.

This suggestion has not been linked to any psychological evidence and therefore seems to lack any psychological substance. As a consequence, it seems to be a slightly lame suggestion, which in all fairness, the candidate seems to appreciate in their evaluation. However, it will lose marks due to the lack of explicit psychology.

Applications	Band 2: The suggestions apply appropriate psychological knowledge explicitly to issues / assumptions raised in the source. They are based on psychological evidence, related to the source and show some pragmatic understanding or evaluation.	Actual marks: 5 out of a maximum 10

This is not references, but actually a bibliography (i.e. which book(s) the candidate has read) thus preventing the candidate from hitting the top band. Additionally, the lack of conciseness in some areas has put the candidate over the word count – it is 1100 words.

Presentation and Communication	Band 2: The assignment is concise and coherent, using a range of psychological terms accurately. References are noted in the text and supplied in the standard format, but there may be minor errors and omissions.	Actual marks: 2 out of a maximum 6

TOTAL MARKS
24/40

QUIZ 5

Experimental control

1. Explain the difference between an experimental group and a control group. [3]

2. Explain the difference between an experimental group and an experimental condition. [3]

3. In what way are standardised instructions important for experimental control? [2]

4. What is it that the standardised procedures are controlling. [2]

5. Suggest **two** ways in which an experimenter might allocate participants to experimental groups. [2 + 2]

6. Why is counterbalancing used? [2]

7. Describe **one** way of counterbalancing conditions. [3]

8. Name **three** kinds of experimental design. [3]

9. What are demand characteristics and why do they matter? [2]

10. Which experimental design(s) avoid order effects? [1]

11. Which experimental design(s) control participant variables? [1]

12. Which experimental design(s) avoid participants guessing the purpose of the study? [1]

13. Name **two** order effects. [2]

14. *A psychological study investigates how caffeine affects memory. The researcher gives participants a memory test before and another one after drinking a cup of coffee. Each test consists of a list of 20 five-letter words. All the words in the lists are equally common.*

    (a) What kind of design was this? [1]

    (b) Which was the experimental condition, and which was the control condition? [2]

    (c) The experimenter used words that were all of similar length and frequency. Give **one** reason why. [2]

    (d) Identify **one** order effect that might affect the result. Explain how. [2]

    (e) Suggest an alternative experimental design that would avoid this. [1]

15. *In an experiment, participants are given two word lists to compare whether it is easier to learn familiar or unfamiliar words.*

    (a) The experimenter wants to ensure that the word lists (one of common words and one of uncommon ones) are equivalent. Suggest **two** methods of doing this. [2]

    (b) If a repeated measures design were used, how could the experimenter counterbalance the lists? [3]

    (c) How might the selection of materials in the study affect the outcome (you can use examples to illustrate your answer)? [3]

16. In an experiment participants are given two word lists to compare whether it is easier to learn 'concrete' or 'abstract' nouns.

    (a) The experimenter wants to ensure that the word lists (one of concrete nouns and one of abstract nouns) are equivalent. Suggest **two** methods of doing this. [2]

    (b) If a repeated measures design was used how could the experimenter counterbalance the lists? [3]

QUIZ 6

Data analysis

1. Susan Morgan asks 20 people to take part in a memory and imagery experiment. Ten participants are tested in Condition A (they are told to just rehearse the words to be recalled) and 10 in Condition B (they are asked to form an image of each word). The numbers of words remembered in each condition were:

   Group A (rehearsal)   4 5 5 7 6 4 6 6 3 8

   Group B (imagery)   6 5 9 6 5 8 7 6 9 7.

   Susan drew two graphs to show her findings

   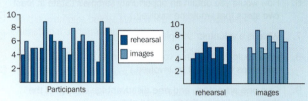

   (a) Which graph is meaningless? Why? [3]

   (b) What information is missing from both charts? [3]

   (c) Are these bar charts or histograms? [1]

   (d) What can you conclude from the graphs? [3]

   (e) Using the raw data, calculate the mean, mode and median for each experimental condition. [3]

   (f) Draw a bar chart of the means alone. Do you think this is a better way to represent the data? Why or why not? [3 + 3]

2. Label the scattergraphs below as positive, negative or zero. [3]

   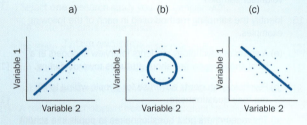

3. What is a correlation coefficient? [2]

4. What is the difference between a correlation and a correlation coefficient? [3]

5. What does a correlation coefficient tell you about a set of data? [2]

6. Give an example of a positive correlation coefficient and a negative correlation coefficient. [2 + 2]

7. Explain what the following correlation coefficients mean:

   (a) +1.00   (d) −0.60

   (b) −1.00   (e) +0.40

   (c) 0.00   (f) +0.10   [2 each]

8. How are correlations used in twin studies? [1]

9. Give **one** advantage and **one** disadvantage of a study using a correlational analysis. [2 + 2]

QUIZ 7

The relationship between researchers and participants

1. Explain why participant reactivity is likely to happen in a study. [2]

2. How could a single blind design overcome the problem of participant reactivity? [2]

3. How could a double blind design overcome the problem of participant reactivity? [2]

4. What is a demand characteristic? [2]

5. In what way does a demand characteristic act as a confounding variable? [2]

6. Give an example of demand characteristics from an investigation you have studied (explain why it is a demand characteristic). [3]

7. Explain investigator bias. [2]

8. Describe **one** way to deal with investigator bias. [2]

9. Explain interviewer bias. [2]

10. What is a participant effect? [2]

11. Identify **one** participant effect and say how you could deal with this effect. [3]

12. *A student designed an experiment that used a repeated measures design to investigate obedience to male and female teachers. The student decided to do this by observing how pupils behaved with different teachers. She asked various friends to record teacher behaviours in their classrooms.*

    (a) State a possible directional hypothesis for this study. [2]

    (b) The student thought it would be a good idea to conduct a pilot study. Describe **two** possible things she could achieve in a pilot study. [2+2]

    (c) Suggest **one** way that investigator bias might be a problem for this study. [2]

    (d) Suggest **one** way that demand characteristics might be a problem for this study. [2]

    (e) What is **one** disadvantage of using undisclosed observation? [2]

13. *Rob Jones designs a set of questions to collect data about people's attitudes about smoking.*

    (a) Explain how he might deal with the problem of response bias when choosing the questions. [2]

    (b) Suggest **one** advantage and **one** disadvantage of presenting the questions in writing rather than conducting face-to-face interviews. [2+2]

    (c) Why would standardised instructions be necessary? [2]

    (d) What is participant reactivity? [2]

    (e) In what way might participant reactivity be a problem in this study? [2]

    (f) How might demand characteristics be a problem in this study? [2]

QUIZ 8

Methods of conducting research

1. Explain the difference between

    (a) A research method and a research design. [3]

    (b) A field experiment and a natural experiment. [3]

    (c) A naturalistic observation and an experiment. [3]

    (d) An investigation using a correlational analysis and an experiment. [3]

    (e) An interview and a questionnaire. [3]

2. Explain why natural experiments are 'quasi-experiments'. [2]

3. Explain why a natural experiment may or may not have greater ecological validity than a laboratory experiment. [3]

4. What is a controlled observation? [2]

5. Explain the difference between disclosed and undisclosed observations. [3]

6. Explain the particular characteristics of a naturalistic observation. [3]

7. In what way can cross-cultural studies be classified as a natural experiment? [3]

8. Give **one** advantage and **one** disadvantage of using interviews as a way of collecting data. [2+2]

9. The person conducting the interviews may have a set of questions that he or she will ask. What kind of interview is this (a structured or unstructured interview)? [1]

10. If you were going to collect data about day care experiences using a questionnaire, write **one** question that would collect quantitative data and **one** question that would elicit qualitative data. [2+2]

11. Why might it be better to conduct an interview than a questionnaire? [3]

12. In the following list, state what research method could be used:

    (a) A researcher records the behaviour of male and female birds during courtship. [1]

    (b) An investigation to demonstrate that rats in a maze without food will learn the layout as quickly as rats which receive food. [1]

    (c) A study of newborn infants to see if they looked longer at a black or chequered square. [1]

    (d) A researcher uses a charity collecting tin to see whether people will give more money if the researcher has a child with him. [1]

    (e) An investigation to look at the relationship between IQ and age. [1]

    (f) A study using the exam results from two schools to see whether streaming (used in school A) was better than no streaming (used in school B). [1]

    (g) A researcher approaches pedestrians and asks them questions about local shopping facilities. [1]

Social psychology: core studies

Milgram (1963) – A behavioural study of obedience

1. This study was really originally intended to be a pilot study. Why did Milgram intend to conduct this pilot study?
2. Identify **two** controls used in this study.
3. Identify **two** deceptions Milgram employed in this study.
4. Consider whether the participants had a genuine right to withdraw in this study.
5. Identify the DV and explain how it was measured.
6. Describe the qualitative data which was collected in Milgram's study.
7. Participants were observed through a one-way mirror. Identify **one** advantage and **one** disadvantage of this technique of collecting data in the context of this study.
8. Describe the sample and sampling method used in this study.
9. Describe **one** advantage and **one** disadvantage of this sampling method.

Piliavin et al. (1969) – Subway Samaritanism

1. Identify the **three** IVs in this study (yes – there are three!).
2. Identify the **four** main victim conditions.
3. Identify the DVs and how they were operationalised.
4. Identify **one** practical problem related to conducting this study.
5. Identify **one** ethical problem related to conducting this study.
6. Consider **two** controls used by the researchers in this study and explain why such controls were considered necessary.
7. Describe the sample used in this study and the sampling method.
8. Identify **one** strength and **one** weakness of this sample.
9. The data were collected mainly through observation. How is this method of data collection better for conducting research on helping behaviour compared to using a questionnaire?
10. Identify some quantitative and some qualitative data collected in this study.
11. Identify **one** advantage and **one** disadvantage of **both** quantitative and qualitative data in the context of this study.

Tajfel (1970) – Experiments in intergroup discrimination

1. Identify Tajfel's aims for this study.
2. Briefly describe the procedures for each of the two experiments.
3. In the first experiment, what is the DV and how was it measured?
4. Write a suitable directional (one-tailed) hypothesis for this first experiment.
5. In the second experiment, what is the DV and how was it measured?
6. Write a suitable directional (one-tailed) hypothesis for this second experiment.
7. Describe the sample and sampling method Tajfel used in this study.
8. Identify **one** advantage and one disadvantage of this sample in the context of this study.
9. Consider **one** ethical issue raised in this study.
10. Consider **two** problems in generalizing the results of this study.

Haney, Banks and Zimbardo (1973) – Prisoners and guards in a simulated prison

1. Identify the IV and DV for this study.
2. The data were collected in several ways. Outline **three** ways that the data were collected.
3. Identify some qualitative and quantitative data which were collected in this study.
4. In relation to this study, identify **one** advantage and **one** disadvantage of qualitative **and** quantitative data.
5. Identify **two** controls which were used in this study.
6. Identify **one** source of bias in this study.
7. Describe the sample and sampling method Zimbardo used in this study.
8. Identify **one** advantage and **one** disadvantage of this sample.
9. Describe **two** ways in which this simulation is quite true to real life.
10. Describe **two** ways in which this simulation is not true to real life.

Developmental psychology: core studies

Samuel and Bryant (1984) – Asking only one question in the conservation experiment

1. Identify the aim of this study.
2. Identify the IVs in this study.
3. Identify the DV.
4. Is this an independent measures, repeated measures or matched pairs design?
5. Describe **one** way in which the findings of this study support Piaget's original findings.
6. Describe **one** way in which the findings of this study do not support Piaget's original findings.
7. Describe the sample Samuel and Bryant used in this study.
8. Identify **one** strength and **one** weakness of this sample.
9. Describe **one** experimental control used in this study.
10. Consider why psychological research (such as this) is sometimes based upon previous research by other psychologists.

Hodges and Tizard (1989) – a study on the effects of privation

1. Explain in what way this study is a natural experiment.
2. Describe **one** advantage of using a natural experiment in the context of this study.
3. Describe **one** disadvantage of using a natural experiment in the context of this study.
4. Identify the IV and DV in this study.
5. Write a suitable hypothesis for this study.
6. Is your hypothesis directional or non-directional?
7. Explain why you choose a directional or non-directional hypothesis.
8. Why do psychologists conduct longitudinal studies?
9. What sampling method was used in this study?
10. Describe **one** disadvantage of this sampling method in the context of this study.
11. Describe how Hodges and Tizard selected the new control group for this study.
12. Explain why Hodges and Tizard had to change the control group sample from their previous research.

Bandura et al. (1961) – Transmission of aggression through imitation of aggressive models

1. Identify the overall aim of this study.
2. Identify the main research method of this study.
3. Who were the participants used in this study? How were they selected?
4. Identify **two** ethical issues raised by this study.
5. What are the IVs in this study?
6. How were the participants matched across the different conditions? Why was this a necessary control?
7. Identify the DV in this study.
8. The data were collected by observation. Describe how the observer collected the data and identify the different categories of observation.
9. Describe what is meant by a double blind technique. Was a double blind technique employed in this study?
10. In relation to this study, identify **one** advantage of observational techniques and **one** disadvantage of observational techniques.
11. This study is a snapshot study. Consider how a longitudinal study may have told us more relevant or useful information.

Freud (1909) – Analysis of a phobia of a 5-year-old boy

1. This study is a case study. What is meant by this term?
2. In relation to this case study, identify **one** advantage and **one** disadvantage of a case study.
3. Most of the data described in Freud's study were collected, not by Freud himself, but by Hans' father. Identify **one** strength in the way that the data were collected and **one** weakness.
4. Identify **one** example of a leading question used by Hans' father.
5. Explain how both Freud and Hans' father may have had a biased view (researcher bias) of Hans' phobia and what effects this may have had on the write-up of the study.
6. Explain in what way the data collected from this study are qualitative.
7. Identify **one** strength and **one** weakness of qualitative data in relation to this study.
8. This study is also a longitudinal study. Consider how it was a strength of this study to investigate Hans' phobia over a period of time.
9. Identify **two** ethical issues raised by this study.

3 A2 specialist choices examination questions

Remember, you will only study **two** out of the **six** possible A2 options.

On each A2 paper, there will be two Section A questions and two Section B questions. You are required to answer **one** Section A question and **one** Section B question.

Some Section A questions in your A2 examinations may target your knowledge of research methods. Here is a taster of the sorts of questions you might encounter.

The following are all examples of Section A questions. Typically, the part (a) will ask you to describe **one** of something.
This should be quite straightforward. The part (b) will ask you to evaluate or discuss something. Here, you will often need to draw upon your knowledge of research methods (especially validity, reliability, bias, participant reactivity as well as perhaps more obvious evaluation issues such as ethics) in order to evaluate the material.

2544: Psychology and Education

1 (a) Describe **one** measurement of learning styles. (6)
1 (b) Discuss the problems of measuring learning styles. (10)

2 (a) Describe **one** psychometric test used in education. (6)
2 (b) Discuss the problems of using psychometric tests. (10)

3 (a) Describe **one** study of the effects of classroom design on performance or mood. (6)
3 (b) Discuss the difficulties of researching the effects of classroom design on performance or mood. (10)

4 (a) Describe **one** way of assessing special educational needs. (6)
4 (b) Discuss the validity of research into special educational needs. (10)

2545: Psychology and Health

1 (a) Describe **one** study investigating patient-practitioner interactions. (6)
1 (b) Evaluate ways of investigating patient-practitioner interactions. (10)

2 (a) Describe **one** way of measuring adherence. (6)
2 (b) Discuss the validity and reliability of measures of adherence. (10)

3 (a) Describe **one** way of controlling pain. (6)
3 (b) Discuss the difficulties of investigating pain-control strategies. (10)

4 (a) Describe **one** study of health promotion. (6)
4 (b) Discuss the ethics of research into health promotion techniques. (10)

2546: Psychology and Organisations

1 (a) Describe **one** type of selection interview for work. (6)
1 (b) Discuss the problems of using interviews as a method for selecting people for work. (10)

2 (a) Describe **one** technique of performance appraisal. (6)
2 (b) Discuss the problems of performance appraisal. (10)

3 (a) Describe **one** way of measuring job satisfaction. (6)
3 (b) Discuss the difficulties of measuring job satisfaction accurately. (10)

4 (a) Describe **one** communication network. (6)
4 (b) Evaluate ways of researching communication networks. (10)

2547: Psychology and Environment

1 (a) Describe **one** study of the negative effects of noise on performance or social relationships. (6)
1 (b) Evaluate the methods used to investigate the negative effects of noise. (10)

2 (a) Describe **one** way of measuring personal space. (6)
2 (b) Evaluate ways of measuring personal space. (10)

3 (a) Describe **one** study of crowds and collective behaviour. (6)
3 (b) Discuss the problems of investigating crowds and collective behaviour. (10)

4 (a) Describe **one** way of measuring environmental cognition. (6)
4 (b) Discuss the validity of measures of environmental cognition. (10)

2548: Psychology and Sport

1 (a) Describe **one** measurement of personality in sport. (6)

1 (b) Discuss the difficulties of measuring personality in sport. (10)

2 (a) Describe **one** study of group cohesion and performance. (6)

2 (b) Discuss the validity of research into group cohesion and performance. (10)

3 (a) Describe **one** study of the use of imagery in sport. (6)

3 (b) Discuss the problems of researching imagery and attention in sport. (10)

4 (a) Discuss **one** type of anxiety in sport. (6)

4 (b) Evaluate the methods of researching anxiety in sport. (10)

2548: Psychology and Crime

1 (a) Describe **one** technique of offender profiling. (6)

1 (b) Discuss the biases and pitfalls of techniques of offender profiling. (10)

2 (a) Describe **one** study of fear of crime. (6)

2 (b) Evaluate the methods of researching for fear of crime. (10)

3 (a) Describe **one** study of morality and crime. (6)

3 (b) Discuss the difficulties of investigatilng morality and crime. (10)

4 (a) Describe **one** study of identification of suspects. (6).

4 (b) Discuss the reliability and validity of methods of identifying suspects.

Many students find the part (b) of these section A essays the most difficult part of the examination. These questions are challenging because they are quite unpredictable and you may feel you have relatively little idea what you are going to face until you turn over your exam paper.

As these question parts are worth 1/5th of each A2 examination, it really is worth doing well on them. It is a very good idea to brainstorm and plan your ideas in the exam before you write. Below is an example brainstorm of one of the health questions on measures of adherence. Spending 5 minutes doing this will set you up to produce an excellent answer.

You can practise doing such plans now:

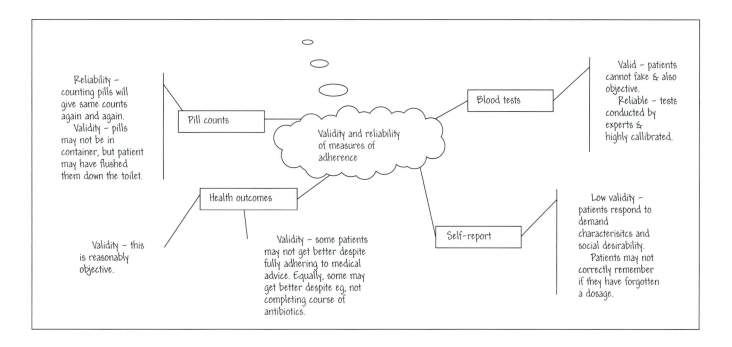

Crossword answers

Across

1. OPERATIONALISATION – Process ensuring that variables are in a form that can be easily tested. (18)
5. INTERVIEW – An investigative method that generally involves a face-to-face interaction with another individual and results in the collection of data. (9)
7. QUALITATIVE – The kind of data that express what people think or feel and cannot be counted. (11)
10. MEAN, MEDIAN – The mode is one measure of central tendency. Name two others. (4,6)
11. MEDIAN – The middle value in a set of scores when they are placed in rank order. (6)
13. STANDARD DEVIATION – A statistical measure of the amount of variation in a set of scores around the mean. (8,9)
21. DOUBLE BLIND – A research design in which neither the participant nor the experimenter is aware of the condition that an individual participant is receiving. (6,5)
22. INTERNAL VALIDITY – The extent to which an observed effect can be attributed to the experimental manipulation rather than some other factor. (8,8)
23. MEAN – The arithmetic average of a group of scores, calculated by dividing the sum of the scores by the number of scores. (4)
24. QUANTITATIVE – Data that represent how much, how long or how many, etc. there are of something; i.e. a behaviour is measured in numbers. (12)
25. COUNTERBALANCING – An experimental technique designed to overcome order and practice effects. (16)
30. INTERNAL – The kind of reliability in which something is consistent within itself; e.g. all test items should be measuring the same thing. (8)
31. MODE – The most frequently occurring score in a set of data. (4)
32. OPPORTUNITY – Kind of sampling in which people are selected who are most easily available at the time of the study. (11)
34. NEGATIVE – A correlation between two variables such that, as the value of one co-variable increases, the other decreases. (8)
35. ORDER EFFECT – In a repeated measures design, a confounding variable arising from the sequence in which conditions are presented, e.g. a practice or fatigue effect. (5,6)
36. IV – In an experiment, the variable that is manipulated by the experimenter (initials). (2)
37. FIELD – An experiment in which the relationship between an independent and dependent variable is studied within the context in which the behaviour normally occurs, (usually) without the participants knowing they are part of a study. (5)
38. DIRECTIONAL – Predicts the kind of difference (e.g. more or less) or relationship (positive or negative) between two groups of participants or between different conditions: hypothesis. (11)
39. HISTOGRAM – A type of frequency distribution in which the number of scores in each category of continuous data are represented by vertical columns. (9)
40. POSITIVE – Kind of correlation in which both variables increase together. (8)

Down

2. RELIABILITY – The extent to which two measures are consistent. (11)
3. BAR CHART – A graph used to represent the frequency of data; the categories on the x axis have no fixed order, and there is no true zero. (3,5)
4. STANDARDISED – Term used to describe instructions or procedures that are the same for all participants to avoid investigator effects and enable replication of the study. (12)
6. EXTERNAL RELIABILITY – A calculation of the extent to which a measure varies from another measure of the same thing. (8,11)
8. METHOD – A way of conducting research in a systematic manner e.g. experiment or interview. Is this the design or the method? (6)
9. RANDOM – A technique for selecting participants such that every member of the population being tested has an equal chance of being selected. (6)
12. CORRELATION – Shows a relationship between two variables. (11)
14. DV – In an experiment, the variable that is measured by the experimenter (initials). (2)
15. PILOT – A small-scale trial of a study run to test any aspects of the design, with a view to making improvements. (5)
16. CORRELATION COEFFICIENT – A number between −1 and +1 that tells us how closely the co-variables in a correlational analysis are related. (11,11)
17. OPEN – In an interview or questionnaire, questions that invite the respondents to provide their own answers rather than select one of those provided. (4)
18. SCATTERGRAPH – A graphical representation of the relationship (i.e. the correlation) between two sets of scores. (12)
19. INDEPENDENT GROUPS – An experimental design in which participants are randomly allocated to two (or more) groups representing different conditions. (11,6)
20. SINGLE BLIND – A type of research design in which the participants are not aware of the research aims or of which condition of the experiment they are receiving. (6,5)
21. DEMAND CHARACTERISTICS – Features of an experiment that a participant unconsciously responds to when searching for clues about how to behave. (6,15)
26. REPEATED MEASURES – A type of experimental design in which each participant takes part in every condition under test. (8,8)
27. RANGE – A measure of dispersion that measures the difference between the highest and lowest score in a set of data. (5)
28. NATURAL – A type of investigation in which the experimenter cannot manipulate the independent variable directly, but in which it varies naturally. (7)
29. VOLUNTEER – A sampling technique that relies solely on people who offer to participate, usually in response to an advertisement. (9)
33. DESIGN – The overall plan of action to maximise meaningful results and minimise ambiguity using research techniques such as control of variables and selection of participants. Is this the design or the method? (6)

Appendix I

Top tips for doing well on your psychological investigations examination

1. Make sure your practical investigations booklet is completely filled in! As about half of your answers may come from this booklet, then to give yourself the best chance, make sure they are filled in correctly.

2. Make sure you have filled in your Blue Peter booklet. This will save you a lot of 'thinking time' (and anguish and stress) in the examination. Also, hopefully, you can show it to your teacher who can check your answers.

3. Your examiner will 'mark positively'. What this means is that should a candidate write the right answer to a question followed by something incorrect, she or he will not lose marks and will be credited for the correct part of the answer. Positive marking is so wonderful that even if a candidate writes the wrong answer followed by the right answer, again, the candidate will receive credit for the right part of the answer. What does this mean for you? It means:

   → If you're in any doubt about what you have written, write something else as well! You are in a win-win situation!

4. YOUR is a four-lettered word! If a question asks, for example, 'Describe one weakness in the way that you selected your sample'... or "Identify one way you could improve your procedure"... or any other question with that special word 'YOUR' in it, then you must clearly and obviously contextualise your answer in terms of the study which **you** carried out. The examiner reading your script will want your answer to be unique and specific to **your** study and not something which any examination candidate might say.

Anyone could write this....(and it would not get many marks!).

> One way I could improve my procedure is that I would use a bigger sample....

But only someone who had really carried out their own Stroop experiment might start to answer their question like this! This answer would get full marks.

> One way I could improve my procedure is that I would give the participants a little practice on the Stroop test before I started timing them. This is because some of the participants took longer because they did not really understand what I required them to do. Therefore, I would give them three colour words to identify the colour to verify their understanding before I started timing them.

5. Timing in the exam.

   → Time is short. You have only one hour to prove yourself. Strong candidates use all of this time and do not take things easy at the beginning of the examination.

   → OK, time is short, but one vital use of time is to read all the questions in each section in advance. This will save you falling into one of two common traps that often occur in the following sort of question:

> (a) Briefly describe **one** weakness in the way that you conducted your investigation. (3)
>
> (b) Briefly describe **one** way of overcoming this weakness. (3)

→ You answer part (a) about identifying a weakness in your study and then you get to part (b) and realize you do not know how to remedy the weakness you have just written about in part (a)!

→ You start writing about how to remedy your weakness in part (a) rather than where it should be in (b). In this case, the material will not receive credit as it is *not* written under part (b). *Remember, each answer is marked independently of another; so each of your answers should be 'stand alone' and not depend on information that you have written down elsewhere.*

Appendix II Inferential statistics:

Why use Inferential Statistics?

Psychologists can draw conclusions from **descriptive statistics** (such as bar charts), in the way that you will have done in your AS coursework – you can see from a graph that one group did better than another group. But was this difference significant? Remember that significance is the extent to which something is particularly unusual.

Consider the following example*: At my local chippy I am convinced that they save money by giving some people rather thinner chips (means they can get more chips from each potato). I know there are two chip bins under the counter – they claim they are the same but I wonder if they are different. So I (sadly) tried an experiment. I asked for one bag of chips from bin 1 and one lot from bin 2, and I went home and measured the width of the chips in each bag.

The null hypothesis is 'The two bins contain chips of an equal average width'.
The alternative hypothesis is 'One bin has thinner chips on average than the other'.

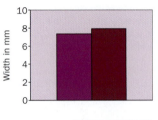

Graph showing the mean width for both bins

There was a very small difference between the average width of each bag (as you can see below) but nothing to write home about. We would expect small differences between samples (bags of chips) just because things do vary a little each time you do them – simply random variation or 'chance'. What we are looking for is a sufficiently large (significant) difference between samples to be sure that the bins are actually different. Otherwise we assume the bins (populations) are the same (accept the null hypothesis).

*Another gem from Hugh Coolican!

Width of chips in mm																						Mean
Bin 1 (fat chips)	4	4	5	5	6	7	7	7	7	8	8	8	8	8	9	9	9	9	9	10		7.35
Bin 2 (thin chips)	5	6	6	7	7	7	7	7	8	8	8	8	8	9	9	9	9	10	10	11		7.95

Significance levels and chance

What inferential statistics allow psychologists to do is draw conclusions based on the probability that a particular pattern of results could have arisen by chance.
If it could have done, then it would be incorrect to conclude that the pattern in the data was caused by the independent variable or to conclude that there was a real correlation between two variables. If it could not have arisen by chance, then the pattern is described as a **significant** one.

Inferential tests of significance are based on some cunning maths that you don't need to know about. They permit you to work out, at a given probability, whether a pattern in the data from a study could have arisen by **chance** or whether the effect occurred because there is a real difference/correlation in the populations from which the samples were drawn.

But what do we mean by 'chance'? We simply decide on a **probability** that we will 'risk'. You can't be certain that an observed effect was not due to chance but you can state how certain you are. In general, psychologists use a probability of $p \leq 0.05$, this means that there is a 5% possibility that the results did occur by chance, in other words – a 5% probability of the results occurring if there is no real difference/association between the populations from which the samples were drawn (the samples may differ but what we are really interested in is knowing how likely it is that the populations must be different).

In some studies psychologists want to be more certain – such as when they are conducting a replication of a previous study or considering the effects of a new drug on health. Then, researchers use a more stringent probability, such as $p \leq 0.01$ or even $p \leq 0.001$. This chosen value of 'p' is called the **significance level**.

Qs 39

1. What letter is used to signify the significance level?

2. What is meant by the phrase 'significant at $p \leq 0.05$'?

3. Suggest why a researcher may choose to use $p \leq 0.01$ in preference to $p \leq 0.05$.

Deciding which inferential test to use

There are three pieces of information you need to know before deciding which inferential test is suitable for your data:

1. Are you looking to find out if your two samples are different or correlated?

2. Are your samples related (e.g. a repeated measures design was used) or are they independent (i.e. an independent groups design was used?

3. What level of measurement was used? (This is explained on the right.)

Which test?

Design/Data	Nominal data	Ordinal data
Association/Correlation	Association: chi-square test (see page 138)	Correlation: Spearman's (see page 139)
Independent samples	chi-square test	Mann–Whitney (see page 140)
Repeated measures (and matched pairs)	Sign test (see page 142)	Wilcoxon (see page 141)

Qs 40

1. With the following designs and data, which test should you use?

   a. An experiment with nominal data and an independent groups design.

   b. An experiment with ratio data and a repeated measures design.

   c. Ordinal data on both measures in a study to see if two measures are associated.

   d. Interval data collected from an experiment with a matched pairs design.

   e. An experiment with an independent groups design in which the DV is measured on a ratio scale.

   f. A study using a correlational technique in which one measure is ordinal and the other is ratio.

   g. A field experiment producing nominal data with an independent groups design.

   h. A study testing an association using a nominal level of measurement.

   i. A study using a correlational technique in which one measure is ratio and the other is ordinal.

2. What is the general name for the value that is worked out using an inferential test?

3. What is the general name given to the number, found in a significance table, that is used to judge the observed value produced by an inferential test?

4. What three pieces of information are needed to find this value?

Levels of measurement

What are nominal, ordinal, interval and ratio data?

Nominal. The data are in separate categories, such as grouping people according to their favourite football team (e.g. Liverpool, Inverness Caledonian Thistle, etc.).

Ordinal. Data are ordered in some way, e.g. asking people to put a list of football teams in order of liking. Liverpool might be first, followed by Inverness, etc. The 'difference' between each item is not the same; i.e. the individual may like the first item a lot more than the second, but there might be only a small difference between the items ranked as second and third.

Interval. Data are measured using units of equal intervals, such as when counting correct answers or using any 'public' unit of measurement. Many psychological studies use *plastic interval scales* in which the intervals are arbitrarily determined so we cannot actually know for certain that there are equal intervals between the numbers. However, for the purposes of analysis, such data may be accepted as interval.

Ratio. There is a true zero point and equal interval between points on the scale, as in most measures of physical quantities such as cm or seconds.

NOIR is the best way to remember all four levels of measurement.

Understanding observed and critical values

Each inferential test produces a single number, the test statistic or **observed value** (so called because it is based on the observations made). To decide if this observed value is significant this figure is compared with another number, found in a table of critical values; this is called the **calculated** or **critical value**. There are different tables of critical values for each different inferential test (see for example page 138). To find the appropriate critical value in a table you need to know several pieces of information about the data:

- the number of participants in the study (N). In studies using an independent groups design there are two values for N – which may be different – they are called N_1 and N_2. In other situations, *df* (degrees of freedom) is used instead of N, and is calculated easily)

- whether the hypothesis was one-or two-tailed

- the significance level e.g. $p \le 0.05$.

When looking up critical values you need to be sure that you are using the correct table and that you are following the right column and row.

Finally, some tests are significant when the observed value is equal to or exceeds the critical value: for others it is the reverse (the size of the difference between the two is irrelevant).

Bigger or smaller?

The observed value should be **greater** than the critical value for:

Spearman, Pearson, chi-square test, related t-test, Unrelated t-test (each test name, like the word 'greater' has a letter 'r')

The observed value should be **less** than the critical value for:

Wilcoxon, Mann-Whitney, Sign (there is no letter 'r' to be found!)

Chi-square (χ^2)

When to use the chi-square test

The hypothesis predicts a *difference* between two conditions or an *association* between variables.

The sets of data must be *independent* (no individual should have a score in more than one 'cell').

The data are in frequencies (*nominal* – see previous page for an explanation).

Note
This test is unreliable when the *expected* frequencies fall below 5 in any cell, i.e. you need at least 20 participants for a 2×2 contingency table.

Critical values of chi-square (χ^2) at the 5% level

df	One-tailed test	Two-tailed test
1	2.71	3.84
2	4.60	5.99
3	6.25	7.82
4	7.78	9.49
5	9.24	11.07

The observed value of χ^2 must be **equal to** or **exceed** the critical value in this table for significance to be shown.

Source: abridged from R.A. Fisher and F. Yates (1974) *Statistical tables for biological, agricultural and medical research (6th edition).* Longman.

How to do the chi-square test: Example 1

Alternative hypothesis: Belief in the paranormal (believing or not believing) is related to a correct assessment of coincidence (non-directional, two-tailed).
Null hypothesis: There is no association between belief in the paranormal and correct assessment of coincidence.

STEP 1 Draw up a contingency table (right)
In this case it will be 2×2 (rows first, then columns)

Assessment of chance	Belief in the paranormal		
	High	Low	Totals
Right	5 (cell **A**)	12 (cell **B**)	17
Wrong	10 (cell **C**)	9 (cell **D**)	19
Totals	15	21	36

STEP 2 Find the observed value by comparing observed and expected frequencies for each cell

	Row × column/ total = expected frequency (E)	Subtract expected value from observed value, ignoring signs $\mid(E-O)\mid$	Square previous value $(E-O)^2$	Divide previous value by expected value $(E-O)^2/E$
Cell A	17×15/36 = 7.08	5 – 7.08 = 2.08	4.3264	0.6110
Cell B	17×21/36 = 9.92	12 – 9.92 = 2.08	4.3264	0.4361
Cell C	19×15/36 = 7.92	10 – 7.92 = 2.08	4.3264	0.5463
Cell D	19×21/36 = 11.08	9 – 11.08 = 2.08	4.3264	0.3905
Adding all the values in the final column gives you the observed value of χ^2				1.984

STEP 3 Find the critical value of chi-square
- Calculate degrees of freedom (*df*): calculate (rows – 1) × (columns – 1) = 1
- Look up the value in a table of critical values (on the left)
- For a two-tailed test, *df* = 1, and the critical value of χ^2 ($p \leq 0.05$) = 3.84
- As the observed value (1.984) is less than the critical value (3.84), we must retain the null hypothesis and conclude that there is no association between belief in the paranormal and the correct assessment of coincidence.

Yates's correction appears in some textbooks but is no longer regarded as necessary.

How to do the chi-square test: Example 2 (a larger contingency table)

Alternative hypothesis: Certain parental styles are associated with greater turmoil in adolescence (non-directional, two-tailed).
Null hypothesis: There is no association between parental style and greater turmoil in adolescence.

STEP 1 Draw up a contingency table (right)
In this case, it will be 3×2 (rows first, then columns)

Parental style	Adolescent turmoil		
	High	Low	Totals
Authoritarian	10 (cell **A**)	4 (cell **B**)	14
Democratic	5 (cell **C**)	7 (cell **D**)	12
Laissez-faire	8 (cell **E**)	2 (cell **F**)	10
Totals	23	13	36

STEP 2 Find the observed value of χ^2 by comparing observed and expected frequencies for each cell

	Row × column/total = expected frequency	Subtract expected value from observed value, ignoring signs $\mid(E-O)\mid$	Square the previous value $(E-O)^2$	Divide the previous value by the expected value $(E-O)^2/E$
Cell A	14×23/36 = 8.94	10 – 8.94 = 1.06	1.1236	0.1257
Cell B	14×13/36 = 5.06	4 – 5.06 = –1.06	1.1236	0.2221
Cell C	12×23/36 = 7.67	5 – 7.67 = –2.67	7.1289	0.9294
Cell D	12×13/36 = 4.33	7 – 4.33 = 2.67	7.1289	1.6464
Cell E	10×23/36 = 6.39	8 – 6.39 = 1.61	2.5921	0.4056
Cell F	10×13/36 = 3.61	2 – 3.61 = –1.61	2.5921	0.7180
Adding all the values in the final column gives you the observed value of χ^2				4.0472

STEP 3 Find the critical value of χ^2
- Calculate degrees of freedom (*df*): calculate (rows – 1) × (columns – 1) = 2
- Look up the critical value in a table of critical values (on the left)
- For a two-tailed test, *df* = 2, and the critical value of χ^2 ($p \leq 0.05$) = 5.99
- As the observed value (4.0472) is less than the critical value (5.99), we must retain the null hypothesis and therefore conclude that there is no association between parental style and greater turmoil in adolescence.

Spearman's rank correlation test

When to use Spearman's rank correlation test

The hypothesis predicts a *correlation* between two variables.

The two sets of data are pairs of scores from one person or thing = *related*.

The data are *ordinal* or *interval* (see page 137 for an explanation).

*Charles Edward Spearman
(1863–1945)*

How to do Spearman's rank correlation test

Alternative hypothesis: Participants' recall on a memory test is positively correlated to their GCSE exam performance (directional, one-tailed).

Null hypothesis: There is no correlation between recall on a memory test and GCSE exam performance.

STEP 1 Record the data, rank each co-variable and calculate the difference

Rank A and B separately, from low to high (i.e. the lowest number receives the rank of 1).

If there are two or more scores with the same number (tied ranks), calculate the rank by working out the mean of the ranks that would have been given.

Participant	Memory score (A)	GCSE score (B)	Rank A	Rank B	Difference between rank A and rank B (d)	d^2
1	18	8	10	2.5	7.5	56.25
2	14	16	5.5	9	–3.5	12.25
3	17	10	9	5	4.0	16.0
4	13	9	4	4	0	0
5	10	15	3	8	–5.0	25.0
6	8	14	1	7	–6.0	36.0
7	15	12	7	6	1	1.0
8	16	8	8	2.5	5.5	30.25
9	9	17	2	10	–8.0	64.0
10	14	5	5.5	1	4.5	20.25
$N = 10$					Σd^2 (sum of differences squared) = 261.0	

STEP 2 Find the observed value of *rho*

$$rho = 1 - \left(\frac{6\Sigma d^2}{N(N^2 - 1)} \right)$$

$$= 1 - \frac{6 \times 261.0}{10 \times (100 - 1)} \qquad = 1 - 1566/990 \qquad = 1 - 1.58 \qquad = -0.58$$

Note that this is a negative correlation – when comparing this figure to the critical value, only the value, not the sign, is important. The sign does, however, tell you whether the correlation is positive or negative. If the prediction was one-tailed and the sign (and therefore the correlation) is not as predicted, then the null hypothesis must be retained.

STEP 3 Find the critical value of *rho*
- $N = 10$
- Look up the critical value in a table of critical values (on the right)
- For a one-tailed test, $N = 10$, and the critical value of *rho* = 0.564
- As the observed value (0.58) is greater than the critical value (0.564) *we should be able to reject the null hypothesis* HOWEVER the sign is in the wrong direction - it is negative whereas we predicted a positive correlation. Therefore we must retain the null hypothesis and conclude that there is no correlation between recall on a memory test and GCSE exam performance.

Critical values of *rho* at 5% level

N	One-tailed test	Two-tailed test
4	1.000	
5	0.900	1.000
6	0.829	0.886
7	0.714	0.786
8	0.643	0.738
9	0.600	0.700
10	0.564	0.648
11	0.536	0.618
12	0.503	0.587
13	0.484	0.560
14	0.464	0.538
15	0.443	0.521
16	0.429	0.503
17	0.414	0.485
18	0.401	0.472
19	0.391	0.460
20	0.380	0.447
21	0.370	0.435
22	0.361	0.425
23	0.353	0.415
24	0.344	0.406
25	0.337	0.398
26	0.331	0.390
27	0.324	0.382
28	0.317	0.375
29	0.312	0.368
30	0.306	0.362

The observed value of *rho* must be **equal to** or **greater than** the critical value in this table for significance to be shown.

Source: J.H. Zhar (1972) Significance testing of the Spearman rank correlation coefficient. Reproduced from the *Journal of the American Statistical Association*, **67**, 578–80. With kind permission of the publisher.

Mann-Whitney *U* test

When to use the Mann-Whitney test

The hypothesis predicts a *difference* between two sets of data.

The two sets of data are from separate groups of participants = *independent groups*.

The data are *ordinal* or *interval* (see page 137 for an explanation).

NB When you have a directional hypothesis, remember to check whether the difference is in the direction that you predicted. If it is not, you cannot reject the null hypothesis.

How to do the Mann–Whitney test

Alternative hypothesis: Male participants interviewed on a high bridge give higher ratings of the attractiveness of a female interviewer than those interviewed on a low bridge (directional, one-tailed).

Null hypothesis: There is no difference in the ratings of attractiveness between those interviewed on a high or low bridge.

STEP 1 Record the data and allocate points

Attractiveness ratings given by high-bridge group	Points	Attractiveness ratings given by low-bridge group	Points
7	1.5	4	0
10	0	6	0.5
8	1.0	2	10.0
6	3.5	5	9.5
5	7.0	3	10.0
8	1.0	5	9.5
9	0.5	6	8.5
7	1.5	4	10.0
10	0	5	9.5
9	0.5	7	7.0
		9	3.0
		3	10.0
		5	9.5
		6	8.5
$N_1 = 10$	16.5	$N_2 = 14$	123.5

To allocate points, consider each score one at a time

Compare this score with all the scores in the other group

Give 1 point for every higher score

Give ½ point for every equal score

STEP 2 Find the observed value of *U*

U is the lowest total number of points

STEP 3 Find the critical value of *U*
- N_1 = number of participants in one group
- N_2 = number of participants in other group
- Look up the critical value in a table of critical values (on the right)
- For a one-tailed test, $N_1 = 10$ and $N_2 = 14$, and the critical value of $U = 41$
- As the observed value (5) is less than the critical value (41), we can reject the null hypothesis and conclude that participants interviewed on a high bridge give higher ratings of attractiveness to a female interviewer than those interviewed on a low bridge.

Critical values of *U* at the 5% level for a one-tailed test

		N_1													
		2	3	4	5	6	7	8	9	10	11	12	13	14	15
N_2	2				0	0	0	1	1	1	1	2	2	2	3
	3		0	0	1	2	2	3	3	4	5	5	6	7	7
	4		0	1	2	3	4	5	6	7	8	9	10	11	12
	5	0	1	2	4	5	6	8	9	11	12	13	15	16	18
	6	0	2	3	5	7	8	10	12	14	16	17	19	21	23
	7	0	2	4	6	8	11	13	15	17	19	21	24	26	28
	8	1	3	5	8	10	13	15	18	20	23	26	28	31	33
	9	1	3	6	9	12	15	18	21	24	27	30	33	36	39
	10	1	4	7	11	14	17	20	24	27	31	34	37	41	44
	11	1	5	8	12	16	19	23	27	31	34	38	42	46	50
	12	2	5	9	13	17	21	26	30	34	38	42	47	51	55
	13	2	6	10	15	19	24	28	33	37	42	47	51	56	61
	14	2	7	11	16	21	26	31	36	41	46	51	56	61	66
	15	3	7	12	18	23	28	33	39	44	50	55	61	66	72

For any N_1 and N_2, the observed value of *U* must be **equal to** or **less than** the critical value in this table for significance to be shown.

Source: R. Runyon and A. Haber (1976) *Fundamentals of behavioural statistics (3rd edition)*. Copyright 1976. Reproduced with kind permission from McGraw-Hill Education.

Critical values of *U* at the 5% level for a two-tailed test

		N_1													
		2	3	4	5	6	7	8	9	10	11	12	13	14	15
N_2	2							0	0	0	0	1	1	1	1
	3				0	1	1	2	2	3	3	4	4	5	5
	4			0	1	2	3	4	4	5	6	7	8	9	10
	5		0	1	2	3	5	6	7	8	9	11	12	13	14
	6		1	2	3	5	6	8	10	11	13	14	16	17	19
	7		1	3	5	6	8	10	12	14	16	18	20	22	24
	8	0	2	4	6	8	10	13	15	17	19	22	24	26	29
	9	0	2	4	7	10	12	15	17	20	23	26	28	31	34
	10	0	3	5	8	11	14	17	20	23	26	29	33	36	39
	11	0	3	6	9	13	16	19	23	26	30	33	37	40	44
	12	1	4	7	11	14	18	22	26	29	33	37	41	45	49
	13	1	4	8	12	16	20	24	28	33	37	41	45	50	54
	14	1	5	9	13	17	22	26	31	36	40	45	50	55	59
	15	1	5	10	14	19	24	29	34	39	44	49	54	59	64

For any N_1 and N_2, the observed value of *U* must be **equal to** or **less than** the critical value in this table for significance to be shown.

Source: R. Runyon and A. Haber (1976) *Fundamentals of behavioural statistics (3rd edition)*. Copyright 1976. Reproduced with kind permission from McGraw-Hill Education.

Wilcoxon matched pairs signed ranks test

Frank Wilcoxon (1892-1965)

When to use the Wilcoxon test

The hypothesis predicts a *difference* between two sets of data.

The two sets of data are pairs of scores from one person (or a matched pair) = *related*.

The data are *ordinal* or *interval* (see page 137 for an explanation).

How to do the Wilcoxon test

Alternative hypothesis: There is a difference in the score on a short-term memory test when it is taken in the morning or in the afternoon (non-directional, two-tailed).

Null hypothesis: There is no difference in the score on a short-term memory test when it is taken in the morning or in the afternoon.

STEP 1 Record the data, calculate the difference between the scores and rank them

Rank the numbers from low to high, ignoring the signs (i.e. the lowest number receives the rank of 1)

If there are two or more of the same number (tied ranks), calculate the rank by working out the mean of the ranks that would have been given.

If the difference is zero, omit this from the ranking and reduce N accordingly.

Participant	Score on test taken in morning	Score on test taken in afternoon	Difference	Rank
1	15	12	3	8
2	14	15	−1	2
3	6	8	−2	5.5
4	15	15	omit	
5	16	12	2	5.5
6	10	14	−4	9
7	8	10	−2	5.5
8	16	15	1	2
9	17	19	−2	5.5
10	16	17	−1	2
11	10	15	−5	10
12	14	8	6	11

STEP 2 Find the observed value of T

T = the sum of the *ranks* of the less frequent sign

In this case, the less frequent sign is plus, so $T = 8 + 5.5 + 2 + 11 = 26.5$

STEP 3 Find the critical value of T

- $N = 11$
- Look up the critical value in a table of critical values (on the right)
- For a two-tailed test, $N = 11$, and the critical value of $T = 10$
- As the observed value (26.5) is greater than the critical value (10), we can retain the null hypothesis and conclude that there is no difference in the score on a short-term memory test when it is taken in the morning or in the afternoon.

Critical values of *T* at the 5% level

N	One-tailed test	Two-tailed test
5	$T \leqslant 0$	
6	2	0
7	3	2
8	5	3
9	8	5
10	11	8
11	13	10
12	17	13
13	21	17
14	25	21
15	30	25
16	35	29
17	41	34
18	47	40
19	53	46
20	60	52
21	67	58
22	75	65
23	83	73
24	91	81
25	100	89
26	110	98
27	119	107
28	130	116
29	141	125
30	151	137
31	163	147
32	175	159
33	187	170

The observed value of T must be **equal to** or **less than** the critical value in this table for significance to be shown.

Source: R. Meddis (1975) *Statistical handbook for non-statisticians.* Copyright 1976. Reproduced with kind permission from McGraw-Hill Education.

If you want help with inferential tests that we haven't covered here or further suggestions about coursework, consult:
- M. Cardwell & H. Coolican (2003) *A-Z Psychology: Coursework (2nd edition)*. Handbook. London: Hodder.
- J. Russell & C. Roberts (2001) *Angles on Psychological Research*. Cheltenham: Nelson Thornes.

The Sign test

When to use the sign test

The hypothesis predicts a *difference* between two sets of data or when you have an answer with only two possible values (e.g. yes/no, plus/minus) of response for each participant.

The two sets of data are pairs of scores from one person (or a matched pair) = *related*.

The data are nominal or reduced to *nominal* data, e.g. + and – (as in the table on the right).

Critical values of *S* at the 5% level

N	One-tailed test	Two-tailed test
5	0	
6	0	0
7	0	0
8	1	0
9	1	1
10	1	1
11	2	1
12	2	2
13	3	2
14	3	2
15	3	3
16	4	3
17	4	4
18	5	4
19	5	4
20	5	5
25	7	7
30	10	9
35	12	11

The observed value of *S* must be **equal to** or **less than** the critical value in this table for significance to be shown.

Source: F. Clegg (1982) *Simple statistics*. Cambridge University Press. With permission from the publishers.

How to do the sign test

Alternative hypothesis: People sleep more after a day of heavy exercise rather than a day spent resting (directional, one-tailed).

Null hypothesis: There is no difference in the amount of sleep after a day of heavy exercise rather than a day spent resting.

STEP 1 Count the number of each sign

Participant	1	2	3	4	5	6	7	8	9	10	11	12
Hours of sleep after a day of heavy exercise	8	8	7	7	8	8	9	9	7.5	7	8	8
Hours of sleep after a day spent resting	7	8.5	8	9	9.5	7.5	8	9.5	7	7.5	8.5	9
Difference	+	-	-	-	-	+	+	-	+	-	-	-

There are 4 pluses and 8 minuses.

STEP 2 Find the observed value of S

S = the less frequently occurring sign, in this case 4

STEP 3 Find the critical value of S

- $N = 12$
- Look up the critical value in a table of critical values (on the left).
- For a one-tailed test, $N = 12$, and the critical value of $S = 2$.
- As the observed value (4) is greater than the critical value (2), we must retain the null hypothesis and conclude that there is no difference between amount of sleep after a day of heavy exercise and amount of sleep after a day spent resting.

As long as you can reduce your data to this form, you can use the sign test.

Qs

41

1. A student conducts a study based on previous research. This research suggests that there will be an association between parenting style (authoritarian, authoritative or permissive) and adjustment in adolescence (high, medium or low). She performs a chi-square test on her data. Her contingency table is 3x3 and she obtains an observed value of 8.13. Her hypothesis was two-tailed.

   a. Select an appropriate significance level.

   b. Work out *df*.

   c. Determine the appropriate critical value.

   d. Should she retain or reject her null hypothesis?

   e. What would she do if she had a one-tailed hypothesis?

2. In another study the observed value of chi-square test was 3.16. The contingency table was 2x2. Would the results be significant at $p \leq 0.05$ if the hypothesis was two-tailed?

3. A sign test generates an observed value of 3.

   a. Would this be significant with 10 participants and a one-tailed hypothesis at $p \leq 0.05$?

   b. Would it be significant if there were 20 participants?

4. A researcher suggested that boys might score lower on a personality test than girls, and this was what she found. There were 10 boys and 13 girls in the sample. To see whether there was a significant difference she used an inferential test and calculated an observed value of 2.

   a. What inferential test would she have used?

   b. Would she use a one-tailed or two-tailed test?

   c. Would the results be significant at $p \leq 0.05$?

   d. Should she retain or reject her null hypothesis?

5. In another study, a researcher compares how boys do on two different personality tests. She expects the scores to be different but is not sure which test will produce a higher score. There were 10 boys in the sample. The observed value was 9.

   Answer questions a–d from question 4.

6. A Wilcoxon test generates an observed value of 30. Would this be significant with 15 participants and a one tailed hypothesis at $p \leq 0.05$?

Appendix III Websites

General psychology sites which include research methods

Both sites are full of information, quizzes and links to elsewhere.

psYonline http://psyonline.edgehill.ac.uk/

s-cool http://www.s-cool.co.uk/default.asp

An OCR site and has useful material and good links
http://www.holah.karoo.net/links.htm

Another vast collection of psychology material including research methods
http://psychology.about.com/

Gerry Kegan's site for Scottish Higher Psychology, again full of useful materials
http://www.gerardkeegan.co.uk/

Gary Sturt's site is a nice starting point for OCR psychology:
http://homepage.ntlworld.com/gary.sturt/gary.htm

A site developed specifically for its own OCR psychology students:
http://www.longroad.ac.uk/accreditation/subject_psychology/index.htm

Research methods

An interactive site for learning about research methods
http://www.mcli.dist.maricopa.edu/proj/res_meth/index.html

syNAPse, the A-Level psychology website developed by Northampton & District A-Level Psychology Teachers Group (NAP). The site is packed full of resources and activities to help A-Level students learn about psychology and in particular psychological research methods.
http://nap.northampton.ac.uk/

Psychological research on the net

Site full of links to a vast array of psychology experiments to take part in
http://psych.hanover.edu/Research/exponnet.html

Yahoo list of on-line tests and experiments
http://dir.yahoo.com/Social_Science/Psychology/Research/Tests_and_Experiments/)

Ethical guidelines

APA code http://www.apa.org/ethics/code.html

BPS code www.bps.org.uk/documents/Code.pdf

Descriptive statistics

A nicely presented introduction to descriptive statistics
http://www.mste.uiuc.edu/hill/dstat/dstat.html

Sites where you can try out correlation simulations (and other statistics)

http://www.stattucino.com/berrie/dsl/regression/regression.html

http://davidmlane.com/hyperstat/prediction.html

http://www.ruf.rice.edu/~lane/rvls.html

http://www.statsoft.com/textbook/stathome.html

Observation coding systems and checklists

Checklists, observations forms etc.
http://www.umchs.org/umchsresources/administration/forms/umchsforms.html#education

Coding Rules for the Hall/Van de Castle System of Quantitative Dream Content Analysis
http://psych.ucsc.edu/dreams/Coding/index.html

Questionnaires

Claims to be the world's largest testing centre, tests and questionnaires on everything http://www.queendom.com/

Various health surveys and other scales
http://www.rand.org/health/surveys.html

Site providing access to copyrighted psychological tests that can be downloaded and used by student researchers including dieting beliefs scale and self-esteem scales
http://www.atkinson.yorku.ca/~psyctest/

OCR site

Contains specification, specimen assessment materials, practical investigations folder, coursework mark scheme, forms for coursework, key skills guidance
http://www.ocr.org.uk/OCR/WebSite/docroot/qualifications/qualificationhome/showQualification.do?qual_oid=2065&site=OCR&oid=2065&server=PRODUKTION

A very shy guy goes into a pub and sees a beautiful woman sitting at the bar. After an hour of gathering up his courage, he finally goes over to her and asks, tentatively, 'Um, would you mind if I chatted with you for a while?'

She responds by yelling, at the top of her voice, 'NO! I won't sleep with you tonight!' Everyone in the bar is now staring at them. Naturally, the guy is hopelessly embarrassed and slinks back to his table.

After a few minutes, the woman walks over to him and apologises. She smiles and says, 'I'm sorry if I embarrassed you. You see, I'm a psychology student, and I'm studying how people respond to embarrassing situations.'

To which he responds, at the top of his voice, 'What do you mean £200?!'

Glossary

Words in *italics* are words that are explained elsewhere in the glossary.

An edited version of this glossary can be found in OCR supplementary materials on the Nelson Thornes website, www.nelsonthornes.com/researchmethods, so that you can make the definitions into a game – paste the descriptions onto cards and then ask students to identify what terms are being defined.

ABBA A form of *counterbalancing* to deal with *order effects* in which participants do condition A, then B, then B and finally A.

aims A statement of what the researcher(s) intend to find out in a research study, (p. 18).

alternative hypothesis A testable statement about the relationship between two variables. Sometimes called the 'experimental hypothesis'. See *hypothesis* and *research prediction*, (p. 9).

attrition The loss of participants from a study over time. Those participants who are less interested or who have done less well may not be available for re-assessment in a *longitudinal study* or in the second condition of a *repeated measures design*, which means that the remaining sample is biased in favour of those who are more interested/motivated/doing well, (p.60).

availability sampling See *opportunity sample*.

bar chart A graph used to represent the frequency of data; the categories on the *x*-axis have no fixed order, and there is no true zero. See *histogram*, (p. 17).

behaviour checklist A list of the behaviours to be recorded during an observational study. Similar to a *coding system*, (p. 56).

bias A systematic distortion. It is a problem in research studies (e.g. *experimenter bias, interviewer bias, observer bias, sample bias, social desirability bias, volunteer bias*), (p. 12).

boredom effect A kind of *order effect*. In a repeated measures design, participants may do less well on one condition rather than another because they have not completed it first and become 'bored', (p. 11).

case study A research investigation that involves a detailed study of a single individual, institution or event. Case studies provide a rich record of human experience but are hard to generalise from, (p. 60).

clinical method (clinical interview) A form of semi-structured or *unstructured interview* similar to the kind of interview used by a GP, (p. 40).

closed questions In a questionnaire, questions that have a range of answers from which respondents select one. Produces *quantitative data*. Answers are easier to analyse than those for *open questions*, (p. 38).

coding system A systematic method for recording observations in which individual behaviours are given a code for ease of recording. Similar to a *behaviour checklist*, (pp. 53, 56).

conclusions The implications drawn from the findings of a study; what the findings tell us about people in general rather than about the particular participants in a study, (pp. 16, 18).

concurrent validity A form of *validity* related to questionnaires, interviews psychometric tests. It aims to demonstrate the extent to which performance on a test correlates positively with other tests of the same thing. If a test is a good one, we would expect a high *positive correlation*, (p. 45).

confederate An individual in an experiment who is not a real participant and has been instructed how to behave by the investigator/experimenter. May act as the *independent variable*, (p. 15).

confidentiality An *ethical issue* concerned with a participant's right to have personal information protected, (pp. 31, 33, 41, 55).

confounding variable A variable that is not the independent variable under study but may be found to have an effect on the dependent variable, thus confounding the findings of the study. See *extraneous variable*, (pp. 14, 24, 29).

content analysis A kind of *observational study* in which behaviour is observed indirectly in written or verbal material. A detailed analysis is made of, for example, books, diaries or TV programmes. It is possible to count the frequency of particular behaviours using categories, (p. 57).

continuous observation Every instance of a behaviour is recorded in as much detail as possible. This is useful if the behaviours you are interested in do not occur very often, (pp. 53).

control refers to the extent to which any variable is held constant or regulated by a researcher, (pp. 14, 26).

control condition In an experiment, the condition that provides a baseline measure of behaviour without the experimental treatment, so that the effect of the experimental treatment may be assessed. See *experimental condition*, (p. 34).

control group In an experiment, a group of participants who receive no treatment. Their behaviour acts as a baseline against which the effect of the independent variable may be measured. See *experimental group*, (p. 34).

controlled observation A form of investigation in which behaviour is observed but under controlled conditions, in contrast with a *naturalistic observation*, (pp. 52, 60).

correlation (correlational analysis) Determining the extent of a relationship between two variables; *co-variables* may not be linked at all (*zero correlation*), they may both increase together (*positive correlation*), or as one co-variable increases, the other decreases (*negative correlation*). Usually a *linear correlation* is predicted, but the relationship can be *curvilinear*, (pp. 42, 43, 46).

correlation coefficient A number between −1 and +1 that tells us how closely the *co-variables* in a correlational analysis are related, (pp. 42, 43).

counterbalancing An experimental technique designed to overcome *order effects*. Counterbalancing ensures that each condition is tested first or second in equal amounts, (p. 11).

co-variables When one conducts a correlational analysis there is no *independent variable* or *dependent variable* – the two measured variables are called co-variables, (p. 42).

covert observations See *undisclosed observations*.

cross-cultural study A kind of *natural experiment* in which the *IV* is different cultural practices and the *DV* is a behaviour such as attachment. This enables researchers to investigate the effects of culture/socialisation or the possibility of a behaviour being a cultural universal, (pp. 60).

curvilinear correlation A non-linear relationship between *co-variables*. For example, arousal and performance do not have a *linear* (straight line) relationship. Performance on many tasks is depressed when arousal is too high or too low; it is best when arousal is moderate, (p. 46).

debriefing A post-research interview designed to inform participants of the true nature of the study and to restore them to the same state they were in at the start of the experiment. It may also be used to gain useful feedback about the procedures in the study. Debriefing is <u>not</u> an *ethical issue*; it is a means of dealing with ethical issues, (pp. 15, 32, 33).

deception An *ethical issue*, most usually where a participant is not told the true aims of a study (e.g. what participation will involve) and thus cannot give truly *informed consent*, (pp. 30, 33, 41, 55).

demand characteristics Features of an experiment that a participant unconsciously responds to when searching for clues about how to behave. These may act as a *confounding variable*, (pp. 24, 39).

dependent variable (DV) A measurable outcome of the action of the *independent variable* in an experiment, (p. 6).

difference studies Studies in which two groups of participants are compared in terms of a *DV* (such as males versus females, or extroverts versus introverts). This is not a true *experiment* because the apparent *IV* (gender or personality) has not been manipulated, (p. 29).

directional hypothesis Predicts the kind of difference (e.g. more or less) or relationship (positive or negative) between two groups of participants or between different conditions. See *non-directional hypothesis*, (p. 9).

disclosed observations See *undisclosed observations*.

double blind A research design in which neither the participant nor the *experimenter* is aware of the condition that an individual participant is receiving, (p. 24).

DV see *dependent variable*.

ecological validity A form of *validity*, concerning the ability to generalise a research effect beyond the particular setting in which it is demonstrated to other settings. Ecological validity is established by *representativeness* (*mundane realism*) and *generalisability* (to other settings), (pp. 26, 27, 34, 55).

ethical committee A group of people within a research institution that must approve a study before it begins, (pp. 32, 33, 55).

ethical guidelines Concrete, quasi-legal documents that help to guide conduct within psychology by establishing principles for standard practice and competence, (pp. 32, 55).

ethical issues An ethical issue arises in research where there are conflicts between the research goals and the participant's rights, (pp. 15, 30, 31, 32, 33, 41, 55).

event sampling An observational technique in which a count is kept of the number of times a certain behaviour (event) occurs. See *time sampling*, (p. 53).

experiment A *research method* that involves the direct manipulation of an *independent variable* in order to test its possible causal relationship with a *dependent variable*. See *laboratory experiment, field experiment, natural experiment*, (pp. 6, 22).

experimental condition In a repeated measures design, the condition containing the *independent variable*. See *control condition*, (p. 34).

experimental control The use of techniques designed to eliminate the effects of *extraneous variables* in an experiment. See *control*.

experimental design A set of procedures used to control the influence of participant variables in an experiment (*repeated measures design, independent groups design or matched participants design: RIM*), (p. 10).

experimental group In an independent groups design, a group of participants who receive the experimental treatment (the *independent variable*). See *control group*, (p. 34).

experimental hypothesis The *alternative hypothesis* in an experiment, (p. 9).

experimental realism The extent to which participants take an experiment seriously. If the simulated task environment is sufficiently engaging, the participants pay attention to the task and not to the fact that they are being observed, thus reducing *participant reactivity*, (p. 24).

experimental validity Concerns the legitimacy of an *experiment* – the way in which it is carried out, the conclusion(s) drawn and its implications for understanding related aspects of real life. Includes both *internal* and *external validity*, (p. 24).

experimenter The person who directly interacts with participants when an experiment is carried out. The study may be designed by someone else, called the *investigator*, (p. 14, 25).

experimenter bias The effect that the experimenter's expectations have on the participants and thus on the results of the experiment. See *investigator effect*, (p. 25).

external reliability A calculation of the extent to which a measure varies from another measure of the same thing over time. This can be assessed using the *test-retest* method. See also *reliability*, (p. 45).

extraneous variable In an experiment, any variable other than the *independent variable* that might potentially affect the *dependent variable* and thereby confound the results. If this happens, an extraneous variable becomes a *confounding variable*, (p. 14).

face validity A form of *external validity* related to questionnaires and interviews. The extent to which the items look like what the test claims to measure, (p. 45).

fatigue effect A kind of *order effect*. In a repeated measures design, participants may do less well on one condition rather than another because they have become tired or bored, (p. 11).

field experiment This is a controlled experiment that is conducted outside a laboratory. The key features are that the *independent variable* is still manipulated by the experimenter, and therefore causal relationships can be demonstrated; it is conducted in a more natural setting than a laboratory experiment and may therefore have greater *ecological validity*; and participants are usually unaware that they are participating in an experiment, thus reducing *participant reactivity*, (p. 22, 23, 27, 29, 31).

field study Any study that takes place away from the laboratory and within the context in which the behaviour normally occurs, (p. 22, 26, 52).

findings The factual data produced in a study, *quantitative* or *qualitative* data. *Conclusions* may be drawn from findings *if* the study was *valid* and *reliable*, (p. 18).

forced choice question The participant must choose one item or alternative from (usually) the two offered, (p. 38).

generalisability The degree to which the findings of a particular study can be applied to the *target population*, (pp. 26, 29).

graph A pictorial representation of the relationship between variables, (pp. 17, 18).

Hawthorne effect The tendency for participants to alter their behaviour merely as a result of knowing that they are being observed. It acts as a *confounding variable*, (pp. 22, 23).

histogram A type of frequency distribution in which the number of scores in each category of continuous data are represented by vertical columns. In contrast to a bar chart, the data in a histogram have a true zero and a logical sequence, there are no spaces between the bars, (p. 18).

historical validity A form of *external validity*, concerning the ability to generalise a research effect beyond the particular time period of the study, (p. 26).

homage to formal terms (Coolican, 2004b).The problem that technical terms create an illusion that things are 'black and white'. They aren't. You should focus on the 'general drift' and not be fazed when you find that there are slightly different meanings as your understanding increases, (p. 25).

hypothesis A precise and testable statement about the world, specifically of the relationship between data to be measured. It is a statement about *populations* and not *samples*. Usually derived from a theoretical explanation, (p. 9).

independent groups design An *experimental design* in which participants are allocated to two (or more) groups representing different conditions. Allocation is usually done using *random techniques*. Contrast with *repeated measures design and matched participants design* (RIM), (pp. 10, 11, 12).

independent variable (IV) Some event that is directly manipulated by an experimenter in order to test its effect on another variable (the *dependent variable*), (p. 6).

informed consent An *ethical issue* and an *ethical guideline* in psychological research whereby participants must be given comprehensive information concerning the nature and purpose of a research study and their role in it, in order that they can make an informed decision about whether to participate, (pp. 30, 55, 57).

inter-interviewer reliability The extent to which two interviewers produce the same outcome from an *interview*, (pp. 41, 44).

internal reliability A measure of the extent to which something is consistent within itself. For a psychological test to have high internal reliability, all test items should be measuring the same thing. This can be assessed using the *split-half method*. See also *reliability*, (p. 45).

inter-observer reliability The extent to which there is agreement between two or more observers involved in observations of a behaviour. This is measured by correlating the observations of two or more observers. A general rule is that if (total number of agreements) / (total number of observations) > 0.80, the data have inter-observer reliability, (pp. 55, 57).

inter-rater reliability See *inter-observer reliability*.

interval data Data are measured using units of equal intervals, such as when counting correct answers or using any 'public' unit of measurement. Many psychological studies use *plastic interval scales* in which the intervals are arbitrarily determined so we cannot actually know for certain that there are equal intervals between the numbers. However, for the purposes of analysis, such data may be accepted as interval. Remember NOIR, (pp. 17, 137).

intervening variable A *variable* that comes between two other variables that is used to explain the relationship between the two variables. For example, if a positive correlation is found between ice cream sales and violence, this may be explained by an intervening variable – heat – which causes the increase in violence.

interview A *research method* that involves a face-to-face, 'real-time' interaction with another individual and results in the collection of data. See *structured interview* and *unstructured interview*, (pp. 40, 41, 44, 45).

interviewer bias The effect of an interviewer's expectations, communicated unconsciously, on a respondent's behaviour, (p. 41).

investigator The person who designs a research study and *may* conduct it. In some cases someone else (sometimes referred to as the *experimenter*) is the one who directly interacts with participants. See *investigator effects*, (p. 25).

investigator bias The effect that the investigator's expectations have on the participants and thus on the results of the experiment. See *experimenter bias*.

investigator effect Anything that the investigator/experimenter does which has an effect on a participant's performance in a study other than what was intended. This includes direct effects (as a consequence of the investigator interacting with the participant) and indirect effects (as a consequence of the investigator designing the study). Some people only include direct effects in their definition of an investigator effect – the unconscious cues from the investigator/experimenter. Investigator effects may act as a *confounding variable*. Investigator effects are not the same as *participant effects*. (p. 25)

IV see *independent variable*.

John Henry effect A *control group* might try extra hard to show that the old way is just as good or better than a new approach. This is a form of *participant effect* and a threat to *validity*, (p. 34).

laboratory Any setting (room or other environment) specially fitted out for conducting research. The laboratory is not the only place where scientific experiments can be conducted. It is, however, the ideal place for experiments because it permits maximum control. Laboratories are not used exclusively for experimental research; e.g. *controlled observations* are also conducted in laboratories, (p. 22).

laboratory experiment An experiment carried out in the controlled and specially designed setting of a *laboratory* and that enables the experimenter to draw conclusions about the causal relationship between the *independent* and *dependent variable*. Not all laboratory experiments have low *ecological validity*, although there is usually a balance to be struck between *control* and *generalisability*, (pp. 22, 23, 29).

leading question A question that is phrased in such a way (e.g. 'Don't you agree that...?') that it makes one response more likely than another. The form or content of the question suggests what answer is desired, (p. 38).

Likert scale A means of providing an answer to a question where respondents can indicate the extent to which they agree or disagree with a statement. There are usually five levels ranging from 'strongly agree' through 'neutral' to 'strongly disagree', (p. 38).

linear correlation A systematic relationship between *co-variables* that is defined by a straight line. See *curvilinear correlation*, (p. 46).

longitudinal design A form of *repeated measures design* in which participants are assessed on two or more occasions as they get older. The *IV* is age. See *longitudinal study*, (p. 60).

longitudinal study A study conducted over a long period of time usually to compare the same individual(s) at different ages.

matched participants design An *experimental design* in which pairs of participants are matched in terms of key variables such as age and IQ. One member of each pair is placed in the *experimental group* and the other member in the *control group*, so that *participant variables* are better controlled than is usually the case in an *independent groups design* experiment, (p. 11).

mean A *measure of central tendency*. The arithmetic average of a group of scores, calculated by dividing the sum of the scores by the number of scores. Takes the values of all the data into account (whereas the *mode* and *median* just take all the data into account – but not the values), (p. 17).

measures of central tendency A descriptive statistic that provides information about a 'typical' response for a set of scores. See *mean, median, mode*, (p. 17).

measures of dispersion A descriptive statistic that provides information about how spread out a set of scores are. See *range, standard deviation*, (p. 17).

median A *measure of central tendency*. The middle value in a set of scores when they are placed in rank order, (p. 17).

mode A *measure of central tendency*. The most frequently occurring score in a set of data, (p. 17).

mundane realism Refers to how an experiment mirrors the real word. The simulated task environment is realistic to the degree to which experiences encountered in the environment will occur in the real world, (pp. 23, 26, 29).

natural experiment A *research method* in which the experimenter cannot manipulate the *independent variable* directly, but where it varies naturally and the effect can be observed on a *dependent variable*. Strictly speaking, an experiment involves the deliberate manipulation of an IV by the experimenter, so causal conclusions cannot be drawn from a natural experiment. In addition, participants are not *randomly allocated* to conditions in a natural experiment, which may reduce *validity*. See also *quasi-experiment*, (pp. 28, 29, 57, 60).

naturalistic observation A *research method* carried out in a naturalistic setting, in which the investigator does not interfere in any way but merely observes the behaviours in question, (pp. 52, 54, 57).

negative correlation A relationship between two *co-variables* such that as the value of one co-variable increases, that of the other decreases, (p. 42).

NOIR An acronym to help remember the four levels of measurement of data: *nominal, ordinal, interval* and *ratio*.

nominal data The data are in separate categories, such as grouping people according to their favourite football team (e.g. Liverpool, Inverness Caledonian Thistle, etc.), remember NOIR (pp. 17, 137).

non-directional hypothesis A form of hypothesis that proposes a difference, correlation or association between two variables but does not specify the direction (e.g. more or less, positive or negative) of such a relationship, (p. 9).

non-participant observations Observations made by someone who is not participating in the activity being observed, (p. 54).

normal distribution A symmetrical bell-shaped frequency distribution. This distribution occurs when certain variables are measured, such as IQ or the life of a light bulb. Such 'events' are distributed in such a way that most of the scores are clustered close to the mean.

null hypothesis An assumption that there is no relationship (difference, association, etc.) in the population from which a sample is taken with respect to the variables being studied, (p. 9).

observational study Participants are observed engaging in whatever behaviour is being studied. The observations are recorded. There are *naturalistic observations* and *controlled observations*. Observational methods may also be used in an experiment – in which case observation is a *research technique* instead of a *research method*.

observation techniques The application of systematic methods of observation in an *observational study, experiment* or other study, (p. 53).

observational systems Systematic methods for recording observations such as a *coding system* or *behaviour checklist*, (p. 53).

observer bias In observational studies, there is the danger that observers might 'see' what they expect to see. This reduces the *validity* of the observations, (pp. 55, 57).

one-tailed hypothesis See *directional hypothesis*.

open questions In an interview or questionnaire, questions that invite the respondents to provide their own answers rather than select one of those provided. Open questions tend to produce *qualitative* data. Answers are more difficult to analyse than those for *closed questions*, (p. 38).

operationalisation Ensuring that variables are in a form that can be easily tested. A concept such as 'educational attainment' or 'social development' needs to be specified more clearly if we are going to investigate it in an experiment or observational study. The researcher lists various behaviours that can be measured, for example, 'social development' can be broken down into the following operations: the tendency to seek the company of others, to show enjoyment when with others, to have a number of friends, to display social skills such as negotiating with friends, etc, (pp. 13, 38, 53).

opportunity sample A *sample* of participants produced by selecting people who are most easily available at the time of the study. Sometimes called an availability sample, (p. 12).

order effect In a repeated measures design, a *confounding variable* arising from the order in which conditions are presented, e.g. a *practice effect* or *fatigue effect*. Counteracted by using *counterbalancing*, (p. 11).

ordinal data Data are ordered in some way, e.g. asking people to put a list of football teams in order of liking. Liverpool might be first, followed by Inverness, etc. The 'difference' between each item is not the same; i.e. the individual may like the first item a lot more than the second, but there might only be a small difference between the items ranked second and third. Remember NOIR, (pp. 17, 137).

participant effects A general term used to acknowledge the fact that participants react to cues in an experimental situation and that this may affect the validity of any conclusions drawn from the investigation, for example, *demand characteristics*. Participant effects are not the same as *investigator effects*, (p. 24).

participant observations Observations made by someone who is also participating in the activity being observed, which may affect their objectivity, (p. 54).

participant reactivity The bias in responses that occurs because a participant knows they are being studied. See *participant effects*, (pp. 25, 54).

participant variables Characteristics of individual participants (such as age, intelligence, etc.) that might influence the outcome of a study, (pp. 11, 14).

pilot study A small-scale trial of a study run to test any aspects of the design, with a view to making improvements, (p. 8).

placebo A condition that should have no effect on the behaviour being studied so can be used to separate out the effects of the *IV* from any effects caused merely by receiving *any* treatment, (p. 59).

plastic interval scale See *interval data*.

population All the people in the world. In any study, the sample of participants is drawn from a *target population*, (p. 12).

population validity A form of *external validity*, concerning the extent to which the findings of a study can be *generalised* to other groups of people besides those who took part in the study, (p. 55).

positive correlation A relationship between two *co-variables* such that as the value of one co-variable increases, this is accompanied by a corresponding increase in the other co-variable, (p. 42).

practice effect A kind of *order effect*. In a repeated measures design, participants may do better on one condition rather than another because they have completed it first and are therefore more 'practiced', (p. 11).

presumptive consent A method of dealing with lack of *informed consent* or *deception*, by asking a group of people who are similar to the participants whether they would agree to take part in a study. If this group of people consent to the procedures in the proposed study, it is presumed that the real participants would agree as well, (pp. 32, 33).

privacy An *ethical issue* that refers to a zone of inaccessibility of mind or body and the trust that this will not be 'invaded'. Contrast with *confidentiality*, (pp. 31, 33, 55, 57).

procedures Includes design decisions as well as all the steps taken when a research study is conducted. See *standardised procedures*, (p. 18).

protection from psychological harm An *ethical issue*. During a research study, participants should not experience negative psychological effects, such as lowered self-esteem or emabarrassment, (pp. 30, 32, 33).

qualitative analysis Any form of analysis that focuses more on words (i.e. what participants say) than on other forms of numerical data. Qualitative analyses interpret the *meaning* of an experience to the individual(s) concerned. See *give voice*, *grounded theory* and *thematic analysis*, (p. 40).

qualitative data Data that express a complete account of what people think or feel. Qualitative data cannot be counted or quantified. Qualitative data can be turned into *quantitative data* by placing them in categories, (pp. 38, 40, 54).

quantitative analysis Any form of analysis (e.g. descriptive statistics) that uses numerical data as the basis for investigation and interpretation, (p. 40).

quantitative data Data that represent how much or how long, or how many, etc. there are of something; i.e. a behaviour is measured in numbers or quantities, (pp. 38, 40, 54).

quasi-experiment Experiments that are not true experiments, either because the *IV* is not directly manipulated and/or because participants are not *randomly allocated* to conditions. Therefore, we cannot claim to investigate cause and effect relationships.

questionnaire A *research method* in which data is collected through the use of written are questions, which may be *open* or *closed questions*. Also called a survey, (pp. 38, 39, 41).

questionnaire fallacy The erroneous belief that a questionnaire actually produces a true picture of what people do and think.

quota sample See *stratified sample*.

random allocation Allocating participants to experimental groups or conditions using random techniques, (p. 12).

random sample A *sample* of participants produced by using a *random technique* such that every member of the *target population* being tested has an equal chance of being selected, (p. 12).

random technique Any technique in which there is no systematic attempt to influence the selection or distribution of the items or participants that form part of the investigation, (p. 12).

range A *measure of dispersion* that measures the difference between the highest and lowest score in a set of data, (p. 17).

ratio data There is a true zero point, as in most measures of physical quantities. Remember NOIR. (pp. 17, 137).

reliability A measure of consistency both within a set of scores or items (*internal reliability*) and also over time such that it is possible to obtain the same results on subsequent occasions when the measure is used (*external reliability*). The reliability of an experiment can be determined through *replication*, (pp. 44, 45).

repeated measures design A type of *experimental design* in which each participant takes part in every condition under test. Contrast with *independent groups design* and *matched participants design* (RIM), (pp. 10, 11).

replication The opportunity to repeat an investigation under the same conditions in order to test the *reliability* of its findings, (pp. 26, 44).

representative sample A *sample* selected so that it accurately stands for or represents the *population* being studied, (p. 12, 26).

representativeness The extent to which an experiment mirrors the real world. This is *mundane realism*, (p. 27).

research The process of gaining knowledge through the systematic examination of data derived empirically or theoretically.

research design The overall plan of action to maximise meaningful results and minimise ambiguity using systematic research techniques, (p. 1).

research method A way of conducting research (such as an *experiment* or a *questionnaire*) as distinct from the *research design* of the investigation, (pp. 1, 39, 52).

research prediction A prediction about the outcome of a study based on the *hypothesis*. The research prediction is about *samples*, whereas the hypothesis is about *populations*, (p. 13).

research technique The specific techniques used in a variety of research methods, such as *control* of variables, *sampling* methods and *coding systems*, (pp. 39, 52).

response set A tendency for interviewees to respond in the same way to all questions, regardless of context. This would *bias* their answers, (p. 45).

right to withdraw An *ethical issue* that participants should be able to stop participating in an experiment if they are uncomfortable with the study, (pp. 31, 33).

RIM An acronym to help remember the three experimental designs (*repeated measures*, *independent groups* and *matched participants*).

role play A controlled observation in which participants are asked to imagine how they would behave in certain situations, and act out the part. This method has the advantage of permitting one to study certain behaviours that might be unethical or difficult to find in the real world, (p. 60).

sample A selection of participants taken from the *target population* being studied and intended to be *representative* of that population, (p. 12).

sample bias A particular problem with questionnaire studies as certain types of people are more likely to complete and return the questionnaire.

sampling The process of taking a sample, (pp. 12, 53).

sampling technique/procedure The method used to *sample* participants, such as *random, opportunity* and *volunteer sampling*, or to sample behaviours in an observation such as event or *time sampling*, (pp. 12, 53).

scattergraph A graphical representation of the relationship (i.e. the *correlation*) between two sets of scores, (p. 42).

screw you effect A participant who knows the aims of an experiment deliberately behaves in a way to spoil an experiment. This is a form of *participant effect* and a threat to *validity*, (p. 24).

semantic differential technique A method of assessing attitudes by measuring the affective component using bipolar adjectives. This means that an attitude can be evaluated on a number of different dimensions, whereas the *Likert scale* only represents one dimension of an attitude (agreement or disagreement), (p. 38).

significance A statistical term indicating that the research findings are sufficiently strong to enable us to reject the *null hypothesis* and accept the research hypothesis under test, (p. 43).

single blind A type of *research design* in which the participant is not aware of the research aims or of which condition of the experiment they are receiving, (pp. 11, 24).

social desirability bias A tendency for respondents to answer questions in a way that presents themselves in a better light, (pp. 28, 38, 41).

split-half method A method of determining the *internal reliability* of a test. Test items are split into two halves and the scores on both halves compared. Scores should be similar if the test is reliable, (p. 44).

standard deviation A *measure of dispersion* that shows the amount of variation in a set of scores. It assesses the spread of data around the mean, (p. 17).

standardised instructions A set of instructions that is the same for all participants so as to avoid *investigator effects* caused by different instructions, (p. 14).

standardised procedures A set of *procedures* that are the same for all participants so as to enable *replication* of the study to take place, (p. 14).

stratified sample A *sampling technique* in which groups of participants are selected in proportion to their frequency in the population in order to obtain a *representative sample*. The aim is to identify sections of the population, or strata, that need to be represented in the study. Individuals from those strata are then selected using a *random technique* for the study. If the sample is not randomly selected from the stratum, it is then a *quota sample*, (p. 12).

structured interview Any *interview* in which the questions are decided in advance, (p. 40).

structured observations The researcher uses various 'systems' to organise observations, such as a *sampling technique* and an *observational system*, (p. 53).

studies using a correlational analysis See *correlation*.

survey See *questionnaire*.

systematic sample A method of obtaining a representative sample by selecting every 5th or 10th person. This can be random if the first person is selected using a random method; then you select every 10th person after this, (p. 12).

target population The group of people that the researcher is interested in. The group of people from whom a *sample* is drawn. The group of people about whom *generalisations* can be made, (p. 12).

test-retest method A method used to check *reliability*. The same test or interview is given to the same participants on two occasions to see if the same results are obtained, (p. 44).

thematic analysis A technique used when analysing *qualitative* data. Themes or concepts are identified before starting a piece of research; then responses from an *interview* or *questionnaire* are organised according to these themes.

time sampling An *observational technique* in which the observer records behaviours in a given time frame, e.g. noting what a target individual is doing every 30 seconds. You may select one or more categories from a checklist. See *event sampling*, (p. 53).

two-tailed hypothesis See non-*directional hypothesis*.

undisclosed observations Observing people without their knowledge, e.g. using one-way mirrors. Knowing that your behaviour is being observed is likely to alter your behaviour, (p. 54).

unstructured interview The interview starts out with some general aims and possibly some questions, and lets the interviewee's answers guide subsequent questions, (p. 40).

unstructured observation An observer records all relevant behaviour but has no system. The behaviour to be studied may be largely unpredictable, (p. 53).

validity Refers to the legitimacy of a study, the extent to which the study or measure is really testing what it claims to be testing, (pp. 24, 34, 45, 55).

variables Anything of relevance in a study that can vary or change. See *independent variable* and *dependent variable*, *extraneous* and *confounding variable*.

volunteer An individual who, acting on their own volition, applies to take part in an investigation, (p. 12).

volunteer bias A form of *sampling bias* because *volunteer* participants are usually more highly motivated than randomly selected participants, (p. 12).

volunteer sample A *sample* of participants produced by a *sampling technique* that relies solely on volunteers to make up the sample, (p. 12).

x-axis The horizontal axis on a graph, going across the page. Usually the *IV*.

y-axis The vertical axis on a graph, going up the side of the page. Usually the *DV* or 'frequency'.

zero correlation No relationship (*correlation*) between *co-variables*, (p. 42).

REFERENCES

Baddeley, A. D. and Longman, D. J. A. (1978) The influence of length and frequency on training sessions on the rate of learning type. *Ergonomics*, 21, 627–635, (p. 29).

Bandura, A., Ross, D. and Ross, S. A. (1961) Transmission of aggression through imitation of aggressive models. *Journal of Abnormal and Social Psychology*, 63, 575–582, (pp. 23, 52, 109, 127).

Baron-Cohen, S., Leslie, A. M. and Frith, U. (1985) Does the autistic child have a 'theory of mind'? *Cognition*, 21, 37-46. (pp. 28, 125).

BEO (2004) Behavioural observation, University of Bern http://www.psy.unibe.ch/beob/proj_ex.htm and http://www.psy.unibe.ch/beob/home_e.htm (accessed September 2004), (p. 55).

Bickman, L. (1974) Clothes make the person. *Psychology Today*, 8(4), 48–51, (p. 24).

Brugger, P., Landis, T. and Regard, M. (1990) A 'sheep–goat effect' in repetition avoidance: extra sensory perception as an effect of subjective probability. *British Journal of Psychology*, 81, 455–468, (p. 46).

Charlton, T., Gunter, B. and Hannan, A. (eds) (2000) *Broadcast television effects in a remote community*. Hillsdale, NJ: Lawrence Erlbaum, (p. 28).

Coolican, H. (1996) *Introduction to research methods and statistics in psychology*. London: Hodder & Stoughton, (p. iv).

Coolican, H. (2004a) Personal communication, (p. 25).

Coolican, H. (2004b) *Research methods and statistics in psychology* (3rd edition). London: Hodder & Stoughton, (p. iv).

Crabb, P. B. and Bielawski, D. (1994) The social representation of material culture and gender in children's books. *Sex Roles*, 10(1/2), 65–75, (p. 56).

Craik, F.I.M. and Lockhart, R. S. (1972) Levels of processing: a framework for memory research. *Journal of Verbal Learning and Verbal Behaviour*, 11, 671–684, (p. 80).

Craik, F. I. M. and Tulving, E. (1975) Depth of processing and the retention of words in episodic memory. *Journal of Experimental Psychology*, 104, 268–294, (p. 80).

Delongis, A., Coyne, J.C., Dokof, G., Folkman, S. and Lazarus, R. S. (1982) The impact of daily hassles, uplifts and major life events to health status. *Health Psychology*, 1, 119–136, (p.89).

Dement, W. and Kleitman, N. (1957) The relation of eye movements during sleep to dream activity: An objective method for studying dreaming. *Journal of Experimental Psychology,* 53, 339-346.

Deregowski, J. (1972) Pictorial perception and culture. *Scientific American*, 227, 82–88.

Dicks, H. V. (1972) *Licensed mass murder: a socio-psychological study of some S.S. killers*. New York: Basic Books, (p. 34).

Dollard, J. R., Doob, L. W; Miller, N. E., Mowrer, O. H. and Sears, R. R. (1939) *Frustration and aggression*. New Haven, Conn.: Yale University Press, (pp. 109, 111).

Ekman, P. and Friesen, W. V. (1978) *Manual for the facial action coding system*. Palo Alto, CA: Consulting Psychology Press, (p. 56).

Festinger, L., Riecken, H. W. and Schachter, S. (1956) *When prophecy fails*. Minneapolis: University of Minnesota Press, (p. 68).

Fick, K. (1993). The influence of an animal on social interactions of nursing home residents in a group setting. *American Journal of Occupational Therapy*, 47, 529–534, (p. 53).

Freud, S. (1909) Analysis of a phobia in a five-year-old-boy. In *Pelican Freud Library*, *Vol. 8, Case Histories I* (1997), (p.127).

Freud, S. (1935) *A general introduction to psychoanalysis*. New York: Washington Square Press, (p. 109).

Gardner, B.T. and Gardner, R. A. (1969). Teaching sign language to a chimpanzee. *Science*, 165, 664–672.

Gilligan, C. and Attanucci, J. (1988) Two moral orientations: gender differences and similarities. *Merrill-Palmer Quarterly*, 34, 223–237, (p. 46).

Gould, S. J. (1982) A nation of morons. *New Scientist*, 6 May, 349–352 (an edited extract from *The Mismeasure of Man*. New York: Norton), (p. 129).

Haney, C., Banks, C. and Zimbardo, P. (1973) A study of prisoners and guards in stimulated prison *Naval Research Reviews*, 30(9), 4–17.

Harms, T., Clifford, R. M. and Cryer, D. (1998) *Early childhood environment rating scale*, (revised edn), New York, NY: Teachers College Press (p. 56).

Hodges, J and Tizard, B. (1989) Social and family relationships of ex-institutional adolescents. *Journal of Child Psychology and Psychiatry*, 30 (1), 77–97, (pp. 2, 127).

Hofling, K. C., Brontzman, E., Dalrymple, S., Graves, N. and Pierce, C. M. (1966) An experimental study in the nurse–physician relationship. *Journal of Mental and Nervous Disorders*, 43, 171–178, (p. 2).

Holmes, T. H. and Rahe, R. H. (1967) The social readjustment rating scale. *Journal of Psychosomatic Research*, 11, 213–218, (p. 111).

Hraba, J. and Grant, G. (1970) Black is beautiful: re-examination of racial preference and identification. *Journal of Personality and Social Psychology*, 16, 398-402, (pp. 2, 129).

Jenness, A. (1932) The role of discussion in changing opinion regarding matter of fact. *Journal of Abnormal and Social Psychology*, 27, 279–296, (p. 80).

Jones, W. H., Russell, D. W., and Nickel T. W. (1977) Belief in the Paranormal Scale: an instrument to measure beliefs in magical phenomena and causes. *JSAS Catalogue of Selected Documents in Psychology*, 7:100 (Ms. no. 1577), (p. 48).

Jost, A. (1897). Die assoziationsfestigkeit in iher abhängigkeit von der verteilung der wiederholungen. *Zeitschrift für Psychologie*, 14, 436–472, (p. 27).

Kamarck, T.W., Manuck, S.B. and Jennings, J.R, (1990) Social support reduces cardiovascular reactivity to psychological challenge: A laboratory model. *Psychosomatic Medicine*, 52, 42–58, (p. 111).

Kendrick K. M., da Costa, A. P., Leigh A. E., Hinton, M. R. and Pierce, J. W. (2001) Sheep don't forget a face. *Nature*, 414, 165–166.

Kiecolt-Glaser, J. K., Garner, W., Speicher, C. E., Penn, G. M., Holliday, J. and Glaser, R. (1984) Psychosocial modifiers of immunocompetence in medical students. *Psychomatic Medicine*, 46, 7–14, (p.111).

Kohlberg, L. (1978) Revisions in the theory and practice of moral development. *Directions for Child Development*, 2, 83–88, (p. 40).

Kohn, P. and Macdonald, J. E. (1992). The Survey of Life Experiences: a decontaminated hassles scale for adults. *Journal of Behavioural Medicine*, 15, 221–236, (p. 65).

Lamb, M. E. and Roopnarine, J. L. (1979) Peer influences on sex-role development in preschoolers. *Child Development*, 50, 1219–1222, (p. 52).

Leventhal, H., Watts, J. C. and Pagano, S. (1967) Affects of fear and instructions on how to cope with danger. *Journal of Personality and Social Psychology*, 6 (321), 331–321, (p. 23).

Lewis, M. K. and Hill, A. J. (1998). Food advertising on British children's television: a content analysis and experimental study with nine year olds. *International Journal of Obesity*, 22, 206–214, (p. 57).

Loftus, E. F. and Palmer, J. C. (1974) Reconstruction of automobile destruction: An example of the interaction between language and memory. *Journal of Verbal Learning and Verbal Behaviour* 13, 585–589, (pp.23, 81, 125).

Mandel, D. R. (1998) The obedience alibi: Milgram's account of the Holocaust reconsidered. *Analyse und Krtik: Zeitschrift für Sozialwissenschaften*, 20, 74–94, (p. 34).

Matthews, K. E. and Canon, L. K. (1975) Environmental noise level as a determinant of helping behaviour. *Journal of Personality and Social Psychology*, 32, 571–577, (p.23).

Middlemist, D. R., Knowles, E. S. and Matter, C. F. (1976) Personal space invasions in the lavatory: suggestive evidence for arousal. *Journal of Personality and Social Psychology*, 33, 541–546, (p. 31).

Milgram, S. (1963) Behavioural study of obedience. *Journal of Abnormal and Social Psychology*, 67, 371–378, (p. 27, 30, 31, 126).

Peterson , L. R. and Peterson, M.J. (1959) Short-term retention of individual verbal items. *Journal of Experimental Psychology*, 58, 193–198, (pp. 22, 109, 126).

Piliavin, I. M., Rodin, J. and Piliavin, J. A. (1969) Good Samaritanism: an underground phenomenon. *Journal of Personality and Social Psychology*, 13, 1200–1213, (p. 25).

Raine A, Buchsbaum M., LaCasse L. (1997) Brain abnormalities in murderers indicated by positron emission tomography. *Biol. Psychiatry*, 42 495–508, (pp. 2, 128).

Ramsay, R. and de Groot, W. (1977) A further look at bereavement. Paper presented at EATI conference, Uppsala. Cited in P.E. Hodgkinson (1980) Testing abnormal grief in the bereaved. *The Nursing Times*, 17 January, 126–128, (p. 111).

Rank, S. G. and Jacobsen, C. K. (1977) Hospital nurses' compliance with medication overdose orders: a failure to replicate. *Journal of Health and Social Behaviour*, 18, 188–193, (p. 27).

Roethlisberger, F. J. and Dickson, W. J. (1939) *Management and the worker: an account of a research program conducted by the Western Electric Company, Chicago*. Cambridge, MA: Harvard University Press, (p. 23).

Rosenhan, D.L. (1973) On being sane in insane places. *Science*, 179, 250–258, (pp. 54, 109, 111, 129).

Rosenthal, R. and Fode, K. L. (1963) The effect of experimenter bias on the performance of the albino rat. *Behavioural Science*, 8(3), 183–189, (p. 25).

Ryback, R. S. (1969) The use of the goldfish as a model for alcohol amnesia in man. *Quarterly Journal of Studies on Alcohol*, 30, 877–882, (p. 6).

Samel, J. and Bryant, P. (1984) Asking only one question in the conservation experiment. *Journal of Child Psychology and Psychiatry*, 25(2) 315–318. (pp. 60, 127)

Schachter, S, and Singer, J.E, (1962) Cognitive, social and psychological determinants of emotional state. *Psychological Review*, 69, 379–399. (pp. 2, 15, 128)

Schafer, W. (1992) *Stress management* for *wellness* (2nd edn). Fort Worth, TX: Holt, Rinehart & Winston.

Schellenberg, E.G. (2004). Music lessons enhance IQ. *Psychological Science*, 15, 511–514, (p. 28).

Schultheiss, O.C., Wirth, M. M. and Stanton, S. (2004) Effects of affiliation and power motivation arousal on salivary progesterone and testosterone. *Hormones and Behaviour*, 46(5), 592–599.

Schunk, D. H. (1983) Reward contingencies and the development of children's skills and self-efficacy. *Journal of Educational Psychology*, 75, 511–518, (p. 23).

Skinner, B. F. (1938) *Science and behaviour*. New York: Macmillan, (pp. 109, 111).

Sperry, R. W. (1968) Hemisphere deconnection and unity in conscious awareness. *American Psychologist*, 23, 723–733, (p.128).

Stroop, J. R. (1935) Studies of interference in serial verbal reactions. *Journal of Experimental Psychology*, 18, 643–662, (p. 8).

Thigpen, C. H. and Checkley, H. (1954) A case of multiple personality. *Journal of Abnormal and Social Psychology*, 49, 135–151.

Tajfel, H. (1970) Experiments in intergroup discrimination *Scientific American* 223, 96–105, (pp. 2, 109, 126).

Veitch, R. and Griffitt, W. (1976) Good news, bad news: affective and interpersonal effects. *Journal of Applied Social Psychology*, 6, 69–75, (p. 25).

Waynforth, D. and Dunbar, R. I. M. (1995). Conditional mate choice strategies in humans – evidence from lonely-hearts advertisements. *Behaviour*, 132, 755–779, (p. 57).

Weick, K. E., Gilfillian, D. P. and Keith, T. A. (1973) The effect of composer credibility on orchestra performance. *Sociometry*, 36, 435–462, (p. 6).

White, G. L., Fishbein, S. and Rutstein, J. (1981) Passionate love and the misattribution of arousal. *Journal of Personality and Social Psychology*, 41, 56–62, (p. 6).

Widdowson, E. M. (1951) Mental contentment and physical growth. *Lancet*, 1, 1316–1318, (p. 30).

Williams, T. M. (1985) Implications of a natural experiment in the developed world for research on television in the developing world. *Journal of Cross Cultural Psychology*, 16(3) Special issue, 263–287, (p. 28).

Zajonc, R.B. (1968) Attitudinal effect of mere exposure. *Journal of Personality and Social Psychology (Monograph)*, 9, 1-29, (p.81).

Zimbardo, P.G. (1969) The human choice. Individuation reason and order versus individuation, impulse and chaos. *Nebraska Symposium on Motivation*, 17, 237–307, (p.109).

Zimbardo, P. G., Banks, P. G., Haney, C. and Jaffe, D. (1973) Pirandellian prison: the mind is a formidable jailor. *New York Times Magazine*, 8 April, 38–60, (p. 60).

Zuckerman, M. (1994) *Behavioural expressions and biosocial bases of sensation seeking*. New York: Cambridge University Press, (p. 54).

NOTES

Use these pages to make any notes.